# Poetry across the Curriculum

**Related Titles of Interest**

*Helping Students Learn to Write: An Idea Book for K-7 Teachers*
Joyce C. Bumgardner
0-205-17571-6

*Helping Students Learn to Write Poetry: An Idea Book for Poets of All Ages*
Joyce C. Bumgardner
0-205-26169-8

*Developing Reading and Writing through Author Awareness: Grades 4–8*
Evelyn Krieger
0-205-17355-1

# Poetry across the Curriculum

## An Action Guide for Elementary Teachers

Aaren Yeatts Perry

Allyn and Bacon
Boston • London • Toronto • Sydney • Tokyo • Singapore

A Viacom Company
Needham Heights, MA 02194

Internet: www.abacon.com
America Online: keyword: College Online



***Library of Congress Cataloging-in-Publication Data***

Perry, Aaren Yeatts.
Poetry across the curriculum : an action guide for elementary teachers / Aaren Yeatts Perry.
p. cm.
Includes bibliographical references (p. ) and indexes.
ISBN 0-205-19807-4
1. Poetry—Study and teaching (Elementary) 2. Poetry—Authorship —Study and teaching (Elementary) 3. Interdisciplinary approach in education. I. Title.
LB1575.P45 1997
372.64—dc20 96-42531
CIP

Printed in the United States of America

10 9 8 7 6 5 4 3 2 1 00 99 98 97 96

*This work is dedicated to the memory of Etheridge Knight (1928–1991), an inspirational poet and caring teacher whom I first encountered when he visited my creative writing class in the Shortridge High School for the Performing Arts in Indianapolis, Indiana. Mr. Knight took the scare and sting out of poetry and gave my love of literature a place to live. I wrote the following poem in honor of Etheridge Knight for publication in issue #32/33 of the* Painted Bride Quarterly:

*Mudsong for Mawdad*

From late summer low river
Mississippi mudbanks naked
words from too deep to dry
drove you North up White
Rivers, pushed you, pulled
your words across our eyes.

You were layin' concrete
poems on a chalkboard,
Jeb gigglin', whiskey on your breaths
talkin' prison and verbs in some
Indianapolis high school.

I felt seven and Hoosier dumb.
And then your voice
which had been through everything,
with the Hard Rock drawl,
turned and said, "What you got
to learn about poetry
ain't in no textbook."
The way your tellin' sang spoke magic
and sprung me from that cell.

Now I wish it wasn't history
stole me from that Indy grave.
I sit and damn slow oil slicks
that clog our river veins,
lean on the bar jonesin' for Shine.
I sing the song of circles,
call the sun to salt the wound
and break the venom silence.

I search the healing mudpacked banks
this river's words left wet.
Sandbubbles pop and crawdads click,
"Give back the earthen Etheridge
Voice Father of my poetry."

—**Aaren Yeatts Perry**

# Contents

# Preface

When I began writing this book I had been teaching poetry classes for over ten years. Since high school I had been publishing and performing my poetry. I had crossed oceans to research various poets. I was proud of how poetry had enriched my academic life, and students could sense that. I could walk into just about any classroom and inspire a group of students to write poems. I had researched, improvised, created, or otherwise gathered lesson plans that worked for me and for the students. But elementary teachers were requesting instructional material that they could use when my residency was over. Teachers were excited about the idea of poetry supporting content learning.

A professor at a graduate school of education suggested that his student teachers might benefit from the use of these poetry-writing exercises in their practice. The English department head at Philadelphia Central High School, one of the top-ranked high schools in the country, had been using poetry workshops for years to enrich a curriculum full of magnet-type, applied-learning options. Some of the poems we wrote at Girls' High School in Philadelphia were used to choreograph dance movement and were performed in a public dance concert with the Body Language Dance Company. A principal at an elementary school requested the workshops as a way of strengthening an intense literacy effort. A student for whom English was a second language wrote his first poem in his mother tongue. Developmentally delayed students in a high–low class wrote poems along with the advanced students.

*They Came from Mars (Costume Party)*

They came from Mars, with weird stars.
Round little faces, holes in places.
Five legs, and for arms pegs.

Pink and green skin, some fat, some thin.
Excuse me mister,
Oh my gosh you're my friend's sister!

—Max Goodman (Grade 4)

Elementary students and their parents were holding poetry readings everywhere from coffee houses to one-time crack houses that had been renovated into Vista libraries. And PTOs around the region were bringing poets and artists into their classrooms in an attempt to make their curriculum more multidisciplinary and multicultural.

During this time I witnessed students showing great excitement about writing poetry, and I wanted to document this. Urban and rural students responded with equal vigor. I saw poetry making a practical contribution to improving students' writing skills and general aptitude across a wide range of class, racial, ethnic, and academic performance criteria.

Across the country, poet-in-residence programs were being used by teachers seeking new ways to strengthen student-centered learning. Nationally, curriculum standards and performance guidelines were undergoing major renovations. Locally, I received encouragement from principals and administrators who applauded new teaching methods that could increase student interest in literature and learning.

Of course, poetry in the classroom is not a new concept. We were all taught to appreciate poetry in elementary school. And in the 1970s and 1980s authors of feminist and multicultural poetry were added to the rich canon of classic, modern, and beat poets. In the 1990s much of the new educational philosophy is based on increasing the role of the arts in the curriculum. This book takes things a step further by showing ways of getting the curriculum into the arts.

There are many rationales for using poetry as a curriculum support tool. Art making in response to content learning creates a record of achievement for the student, her peers, and the teacher. Sharing new information in a creative way reinforces comprehension and relevance for the student. Where true learning occurs, the desire to teach is born. And where true teaching is done, the learning lasts.

These workshop suggestions are not meant to be used as a separate elective, like lessons and musical instruments, but are meant to give you some bases from which to begin exploring poetry and from which to further explore classroom and life skills topics through the writing process.

As the instructor, you become the poet. By reading the model poem, you are breathing life into the class. It should be read in such a manner that the students will understand its music, language, intensity, and meaning. This level of student understanding will give you a vehicle to present new material or to expand on a previous lesson.

Poetry presents you with many "teachable moments." Using the model poem approach, you can expose students to art and literature. By studying the life of an author a teacher can encourage social studies or biographical research into just about any area: the place where a poet lived, the social conditions influencing his or her writing, the professional life of the poet, the other professions or occupations of the poet, other writers who influenced or were influenced by the poet.

*Colors*

Colors falling out of the sky
on me. The clothes I wear are yellow,
black, white, red, blue, pink, green, purple
and many more. My world
the colors of the sunset.

—LaMer Steptoe (Grade 4)

Studying the poem itself requires and encourages a range of academic skills. It calls for basic listening and reading skills. Poetry study trains one in many modes of thinking: nonlinear, free thinking; sequential, ordered, critical, and scientific thinking; musical and rhythmic thinking; and philosophical thinking. Poetry also demands the ability to stop thinking, remain quiet, and receive information through other channels. Reading poetry necessitates a high level of empathy and insight into other peoples' lives. Reading it, writing it, and responding to it are examples of applied learning.

There are plenty of concrete goals to set and accomplish: first complete poem, first reading, first published poem, first self-published book, first contest or award won, first fully published collection. As you read and reread your own and others' poems, you will notice new things in your everyday life. The smallest things will seem beautiful and important, and the larger things—the big picture—will seem bigger than ever before.

Poetry meets and crosses elementary school curricula at many junctures. Not the least of these is their fundamental common ground of problem solving. When undertaken as a part of the writing process poetry is a form of linguistic problem solving. Palmer, Hafner, and Sharp (1994) emphasize that "As developing writers move through this [writing] process to produce, eventually, a piece of writing that accurately represents their thoughts, they are problem solving."

Each poem contains a distinct sequential methodology. And it requires a nonlinear creative thinking process, which produces "solutions" as unique as one's DNA. When a student is asked to solve a problem and give an answer in the form of a poem, there is no failure. There is only achievement. By personalizing his or her awareness of a given topic a student is bringing its meaning to life. Until this happens, the simplest mathematic equation or social studies fact will fall into the void of inapplicability and sit untapped in the student's memory. If the student is given permission to create a personal response to knowledge, then new meaning is being constructed. "When students construct meaning as readers and writers," say Palmer, Hafner, and Sharp (1994), "they rely on their past experiences a great deal to make sense of the tasks at hand; they are both building and expressing background knowledge."

*A Word*

A word is a word.
But why is a word a word?

—LaMer Steptoe (Grade 4)

## ACKNOWLEDGMENTS

As teachers, writers, and mentors encouraged my writing as a student, so did colleagues and comrades support me during this project. I am profoundly grateful to the many people who have shown faith in my work and in the educational powers of the arts. Some of them are Bob Adamski, Miguel Algarin, Dan Araco, Judy Ashkenaz, James Baldwin, Julia Blumenreich, William Brown, Dennis Brutus, Dr. Dorothy Burton, Dr. Ken Dossar, Gerry Givnish, David Goodman, Mary Day Kent, Mary Beth Lauer, Elizabeth McKim, Gil Ott, Teresa Leo, the Painted Bride Art Center, the PA Council on the Arts, Jane and Don Perry, the School District of Philadelphia, Larry Robin, Dr. Sonia Sanchez, Dr. Aurora Camacho de Schmidt, Lamont B. Steptoe, Allen Southerland, Grechen Throop, the WPCA, Bryn Walsh, Korben Weyler, and Gaeton Zorzi. I want to thank Cynthia Ferguson, Rebecca Olien, and Clare Lezch for reviewing the manuscript. And most of all, I want to thank the teachers and students whose imagination is what the future is made of.

# INTRODUCTION

## How to Use This Book

This book is an action guide for elementary teachers who want to use poetry in the classroom. It is a compendium of tested poetry-writing exercises. The suggested methodologies are designed to support your students' educational development across standard elementary curricula. The book's purpose is to make it easier for you, as a teacher, to find and use poetry teaching material that is suitable for your classroom.

### HOW TO USE THIS BOOK

To use this book, simply look up a poetry-writing exercise that meets your needs and follow the teaching instructions. Read through the exercise completely before taking it to class, and write a sample poem of your own as preparation for student questions. The exercises are step-by-step lesson plans grouped by curriculum so that you can easily find a writing exercise that relates to your current study unit. For each curricular discipline or content area you will find a whole chapter filled with poetry-writing ideas. These are listed in the table of contents. You may also look up poetry-writing exercises by grade level or subject area as noted in the exercise headings. At the end of the book you also will find a glossary of terminologies and poetic forms.

Unless a specific poetic form is suggested, the poetry writings can take on any form. The thematic content of the exercises will inspire their forms as students experiment. A science poem about volcanoes, for example, can be written in forms like haiku, renga, tanka, cinquaine, or sestina. It may be written in the shape of a volcano or in the child's own form. A limerick about the "man in the moon" may use numbers in a form poem and refer to science and math—but the life of the poem still depends on the individual student's ideas. Some students will write and think more freely when given no form restrictions. Others need a writing assignment that is predictable and formulaic. Most assignments in this book allow for a combination of both.

> *"Form follows function."*—Frank Lloyd Wright (architect)
> *"Form is never more than an extension of content."*
> —Robert Creeley (poet)
> Study Booklet, NAROPA Institute, Boulder, CO 1992

These writing projects can be done in small groups, in a circle, or with all desks facing forward. Most of the writing projects are conducted through dialogue with students. Some can be done in a quiet, contemplative mode. Others are lesson plans for high-energy poetry exchanges. Once you become familiar with the exercise format, you can begin to modify the exercises to fit your desired outcome and your students' performance levels. You can conduct the exercises verbatim, or you can add your personal touch and take them further using the suggestions in Chapter 1. Your level of personal interest in literature and your ingenuity in exploring it with your students will greatly expand their participation in the poetry exercises.

The poetry-writing exercises require a minimum of preparation and support materials. This teacher's action guide recommends the use of standard classroom resources such as student folders, pencils, paper, books, arts and crafts supplies, parents and other volunteers, electronic equipment, imagination, and "model poems."

In each curriculum-based chapter you will find some exercise instructions that suggest optional use of sample or model poems. These are classic, contemporary, and current poems that exemplify the intended poetry lesson in the writing exercise where they are listed. The poems can be found in the well-known anthologies referenced in the notes at the end of each chapter. You will certainly have a lifetime of reading pleasure at your fingertips if you buy these for your own collection. They can also be purchased as permanent additions to your school library.

If the school cannot supply the suggested anthologies, try enlisting the support of a parent or the parent–teacher organization. Parents from one class or grade may be able to buy one book, while another set of parents may contribute a different book to the school library. Explore the possibility of local companies or corporations contributing funds for a poetry center in your library, a poetry oasis in your classroom, or a "Poetree" in your school lobby.

I created some of these exercises during ten years of conducting poetry workshops in public and private elementary classrooms. Several factors influenced my desire to produce such a resource for teachers. I found that there was a shortage of available lesson plans and guide books for teaching poetry, except for the classics. These texts focused either on the nursery rhyme aspects or the college-level technical aspects of poetry. Also I found that many of the teachers whose classrooms I visited were afraid to teach poetry, if only out of respect for it. Either the apparent complexity of good poetry scared teachers away from professing it, or it was presented as a relic of the past. Yet elementary students showed genuine and consistent interest in poetry, and I witnessed academic successes using poetry in the classroom. This led me to the conclusion that poetry can be used to help improve writing, thinking, and academic skills in general.

Process portfolios are also gaining popularity as an improved form of student assessment and evaluation. Keeping a poetry process portfolio can be a learning experience for the student, and building a poetry process portfolio can have a direct and long-term impact on a student's commitment to the writing process.

I have followed the progress of three girls, now in sixth grade, since I was their teacher at an early childhood education center. One of these children was "writing before she could write." That is, she watched her mother writing so often that she imitated her in squiggles that looked something like Arabic or Hebrew letters. Her mother saved these. Another started writing parallel poems in second and third grade in the same style as some of her father's writing. Her father saved these and repeatedly asked her to read them back to him. The third girl was repeatedly praised for her poetry and drawings of animals. All three girls now have self-published books of creative writing!

Granted, all of these girls have loving parents who happen to be writers. But I am convinced that the common element that inspired these students to continue writing was their parents' ability to find a place to keep their artwork and save their writings.

Archiving and presenting are natural tendencies that can be encouraged and developed. Look at the walls of any teenager's bedroom. They are sprawling portfolios of fascinations, aspirations, infatuations, explorations, and memorabilia. Teenagers' walls are mile markers, the signage of who they are and want to be. They may be early declarations of independence along with expressions of the need for continued support.

The act of making and reading poetry can be an effective language acquisition tool and an enjoyable way for students to experience new figures of speech. It can open the floodgates of all modes of expression in short, manageable measures.

The writing exercises in *Poetry across the Curriculum* utilize various modes of language acquisition. Using a *reading* method, students can read poetry of the canon, of self, and of peers to acquire the feel and action of sentence structure and word play without intensely studying its grammar. An *audiolingual* approach of listening and repeating is recommended in many exercises. A *cognitive* approach, using what students know to combine rules-learning and use-based habit formation is also suggested by the use of curriculum content for poem topics. And a *natural* approach is used insofar as the teacher becomes the presenting poet and, for that section of the workshops, allows students to observe and acquire through the teacher's oral presentation.

A boy who had been refusing to participate in class began his reentry into the culture by writing and reading his poems. One teacher was amazed when her third-grade girl, who was practically aphasic, began speaking clearly and unabashedly when she read her poems back. A fourth grader who had been resisting writing began showing improvement after he wrote some of his haiku poems in his first language: Spanish! And I saw incidents of catharsis where students began to confront personal and domestic problems through their poems.

When Etheridge Knight said to me, "What you have to learn about poetry ain't in no textbook," I turned a corner in my journey as teacher and writer. That journey has led to this book. I wanted to see poetry taught as a living art. Poetry, nursery rhyme, and story played this role in every day care center I worked in. I wanted to see the curriculum embrace the affective-learning capacity of poetry. Yet, in the urban and rural classrooms I visited, the sheer excitement and power of poetry as a beautiful expression of humanity and consciousness was lost to those elementary students who most needed it. The poetry of yesterday and today is an apt, even scientific social analysis of our past and can certainly be a guide for our future.

Here I have combined creative-writing teaching strategies with standard elementary school curriculum topics. And I have adopted to primary grade levels some of the best workshop ideas used by poets around the country. Sources are quoted and referenced. Additional poetry and creative writing books for elementary teachers are listed in the bibliography.

For the purposes of this book, the terms *writing exercise, writing project, writing workshop, lesson plan*, and *writing activity* are synonymous. The language of the book is for an audience of elementary school teachers and workshop facilitators. *Students, children*, and *young poets* refer to the students in your classroom or to the participants in your writing workshops. The words *he* and *his* or *she* and *her* are not meant to be gender-exclusive but are used in this text to signify the anonymous second person, as in "No one is happy when he is abandoned" or "Ask each student to give it her best shot."

This book may also be used as a planning guide. A student-teacher, reading assistant, or parent can be asked to locate books or recordings of famous poets reading, to photocopy student poems or type them up, or to help organize an anthology or a community poetry reading. Use the writing ideas as homework assignments, library or after-school activities, or for small reading group assignments. If you have a group of prolific poets in your fifth- or sixth-grade classroom, or if you are in a K–12 school, have older students conduct exercises from this book with younger students as peer poets.

What is poetic? What is poetry? Answers will emerge as you explore these writing exercises. Your training and personal philosophy will color, flavor, or scent your findings and send you up new paths. This action guide contains numerous quotes from noted authors who have created answers to these age-old questions. As you work through the exercises, you may find some quotes that are appropriate to use with your students.

Read Chapter 1 and then try one of the workshop ideas yourself. Have fun with these exercises. And watch poetry become a vital and empowering teaching tool in your classroom.

# ▶ 1

# How to Conduct Poetry Lessons

What follows are easy-to-use guidelines for conducting poetry-writing exercises with elementary students. The guidelines are suggestions based on steps used by experienced poets and teachers. These writing exercises can be conducted in 45- to 60-minute class periods or can be modified to fit your classroom needs.

A typical 60-minute workshop might spend 5 minutes on the introduction, 10 minutes reading and discussing the model poem, 10 minutes brainstorming and writing a group poem on the board as a prewriting sample, 5 minutes explaining and assigning individual poetry writing, 15 to 20 minutes on individual writing, and 10 to 15 minutes for students to read aloud their finished rough drafts. If you have one poetry workshop every week, the next workshop might spend 10 minutes reviewing the previous lesson with another reading of the model poem, 20 to 30 minutes reading the rest of the rough drafts with student feedback and teacher critique, 15 minutes revising rough drafts and editing finished drafts, and 5 to 10 minutes for a reading by a few students with finished revisions.

The steps of the writing exercises are listed sequentially as they should occur in the classroom. They can be extended or limited in length, or spread out over multiple class sessions, depending on your time and goals. The steps are derived from the stages of the writing process: prewriting, rough draft, revision, edit, final draft, peer review, and publishing. The writing exercises recommend drawing on the student and the classroom curriculum for poem content selection. And this book suggests parental and community involvement through readings, publication, and display.

The workshops are multidisciplinary in that their themes and contents cover every curricular area (except computers) from art to zoology. Math-related exercises are included in Chapter 6 (Science/Math). The Social Studies content areas of Human Values and Citizenship are given separate chapters (Chapters 8 and 9, respectively). Chapter 8 on Human Values contains poetry-writing exercises about the life-skills issues of self-esteem, family communication, cultural identity, and social skills. Citizenship writing exercises center primarily around conflict resolution issues. Computers can appear in poetry, but they are referred to here as a resource in publication and display suggestions.

*Poetry across the Curriculum* also recommends the use of a process portfolio throughout and at the end of a series of workshops. A process portfolio is a very active student folder to hold writings and track progress. Some of the writing exercises are primers meant to spark interest and curiosity. Others are more substantive ideas for poems that can be crafted and developed into solid literary entities. Try to take some of the exercises through all the recommended stages so that you can evaluate your process as well as student writing progress.

*Poems*

In poems, our earth's wonders
Are windowed through
        Words
A good poem must haunt the heart
And be heeded by the head of the
        Hearer
With a wave of words, a poet can
Change his feelings into cool, magical, mysterious
        Mirages
Without poetry our world would be
Locked within itself—no longer enchanted by the poet's
        Spell.

—Peter Kelso (Age 11, Australia)[1]

## PLANNING A POETRY LESSON

First, choose a poetry-writing lesson topic. Read through the instructions. As with any lesson plan, make sure that you have gathered all the resources you will need before beginning the workshop. Prepare some sample starter questions for dialogue with the class, both about the poem and about the writing exercise. How much time will you spend on each stage of the workshop? Which student will be your time-keeper if you need one? Which student(s) will be the "scribe," a poetry minute-taker who is assigned to write down the group poems and instructions that you write on the board? You can copy these and hand them out.

Do you have a copy of the model poem? If you cannot obtain a copy of the suggested model poem for the class, you can write your own example poem based on the instructions. Become familiar with the poem in advance. Will reading it aloud suffice? If you want your group to read a printed poem that needs to be duplicated, you may want to copy blank lines onto the other side of the paper for student writing. If the lesson includes reference to a new poetry tool, you can find listings for tools, techniques, and forms in the glossaries.

Teachers of first and second grades can adapt the writing-based exercises by asking students to say words or lines, and writing them on the board. Basic reading, spelling, and language acquisition skills can be increased by having first- and second-grade students see their words materialize before them on the board. Writing suggestions directly into view on the chalkboard is a great way to teach editing. Through questions and dialogue the class can see you trying their suggestions, which validates their responses to your questions. They can see you trusting the process of coming up with the right words, crossing out first words, writing in new words, and ending up with a line that expresses something in a way it has never before been expressed. Furthermore, reading a new poem from the board aloud with the whole class is a fun spelling and word-recognition activity for the early grades.

> *"He who, in an enlightened and literary society, aspires to be a great poet, must first become a little child."*—Macaulay

## SETTING A COURSE

An important first step to a successful poetry workshop is to choose an objective. Being clear about your main objective helps you gauge how much time to spend on other workshops goals. Think through the steps of the workshop and decide what you want to accomplish based on both process and outcome. Begin your workshops by explaining the purpose of today's lesson to the class.

What do you want children to remember most about this lesson? How will you summarize the lesson for students? Is your goal to expose the class to a poem, to discuss a poem, to brainstorm ideas, to write lists for later writing, to review the rules of a form poem, to give everyone a chance to read last week's poem? Or do you want to get a rough draft written so that you can discuss it next week? Most of the exercises are designed so that you can get rough drafts written in one session.

No matter what your goal, the pace you set for your workshops will be an important determinant of the consistency of student participation. Tempering poetic contemplation with intense dialogue requires great focus. The workshops need both. If you set approximate time limits for each workshop segment and watch the clock, a lot can be accomplished in a short time.

## PRESENTING THE POETRY LESSON PLAN TO THE CLASS

Write the name of the lesson plan on the board and on handout sheets if you are using them. Remind the class of the intended purpose of the workshop. Build up student interest by mentioning the workshop name and intention at least a day in advance. Explain the poetry elements to be explored.

If you are presenting a new poetry tool, like onomatopoeia, draw a picture of a toolbox on the board and write the name of any tool or resource in the Poetry Tool Box. This can be a square with lines in it, a representation of a workbench shelf, or an old-fashioned hand-made tool box with a handle.

If there are participation rules for workshops or elements you want students to look out for in a poem, let them know beforehand. Let the class know if it is a listening exercise or a writing exercise. Always say how much time there is.

In laying out the rules for a writing exercise, it is important to be clear, but equally important to be flexible. If a child pays more attention to rules than to creative impulse, then the intention of the workshop is lost. "Often," says Alice Miller, "a child's very gifts (his great intensity of feeling, depth of experience, curiosity, intelligence, quickness—and his ability to be critical) will confront his parents with conflicts that they have long sought to keep at bay with rules and regulations."[2] The role of the teacher as facilitator in the workshop setting is a subtle and challenging one. It involves giving the child plans, directions, and limits. At the same time, it requires patience, flexibility, and insight into your students' circumstances.

In presenting a writing exercise, it sometimes helps to remind students of some of the things that can be done with finished poems.

A poetry activity can begin in the classroom and extend to an imaginary place. Depending on your energy for pretend and ceremony and your students' responsiveness to group focus concepts such as "putting on your thinking cap," you may want to extend the idea of poetry occurring in a protected place. Many classrooms have a Poetry Corner decorated with student work, pictures of famous poets, and the Poetry Tool Box. Depending on your success with visual aides, you may want to try building a "Poetree House," a two-dimensional tree with poetry concepts, forms, and books that you have studied appearing on the branches. The environment in which you conduct the workshops and the display of finished poems can be changed to inspire student imagination.

## PRESENTING A MODEL POEM

Read a model poem to the class. Play a cassette tape. Present objects or photographs. Introduce a complex concept. Walk into the classroom saying a poem loudly and forcefully with no introduction. Stand on a chair and say it. Lie on the floor and say it. Have the class clap a rhythm for you while you say it. Create ceremony and nuance whenever possible. Whatever you have to do to lodge the poem in the creative center of your classroom's collective ear, do it. Honor the poem with a good reading, whether it was written by you or by an author who lived two thousand years ago. This is part of the joy of poetry.

As a teacher facilitating a poetry workshop, you are now a presenting artist. The level of energy you put into exciting your class about a new poem will be similar to the output energy level of their writing. This is especially true with visiting writers in any genre. If a playwright, journalist, or songwriter enters the classroom and begins by talking about the mechanics of their craft or touting their resume, the session will stall. If they begin by reading or performing the work they believe in, the student response is categorically more productive.

This is the most challenging and the most rewarding aspect of this type of teaching. Use poems that excite you, including the ones you write, and your students will in turn be excited about writing.

"Timing is everything" is a maxim that is particularly true in presenting poetry. The speed at which you read the sample poem, the pauses at line breaks and between stanzas, the emphasis on and intonations of important words, the time you allow for contemplation of the poem, and the time you allow for discussion will all contribute to either building energy (for excited writing) or releasing energy (for contemplative writing). And have students take turns reading model poems. If a student reads enough meaningful poems (or any kind of writing), silently or aloud, he or she will begin writing at some point, with or without instruction. As I say repeatedly to students who say they want to write but hate reading: "You cannot write if you do not read."

## USING PLANNED CLASSROOM DISCUSSION

Discussion is the most important prewriting task. It sparks and fuels the student impetus to write. Even without a model poem, an exercise can be started by discussing the topic about which you want students to write. This is one of the methods used in the nonliterate communities Paulo Freire worked with in Brazil when he was writing *Pedagogy of the Oppressed*. Dialogue is the basis for the "problem-posing" strategy of teaching that he recommends: "The teacher is no longer merely the-one-who-teaches, but one who is himself taught in dialogue with the students, who in turn while being taught also teach. They become jointly responsible for a process in which all grow."[3]

If you do have a model poem, begin by discussing how it is relevant to the lives of the students. The more relevant the topic of discussion to the daily life of the student, the greater the learning. A Gwendolyn Brooks poem about a broken window in Chicago and a Robert Frost poem about a wooded path in New England can be equally relevant. Have a short discussion in which you ask your students a predetermined list of starter questions that can bridge the meaning and content of the poem into the classroom: "Have you ever felt like that?" "Who can tell me what the poet means by . . . ?" "How old do you think the boys in that poem are?" If students know that the floor will be open for opinions after each model poem, their listening and comprehension level will go up, their editorial vocabulary will improve, and participation will stay high.

A Poetry Critique Guide Sheet containing jump-starter discussion questions can be passed out or posted. You can call it a Rap Sheet or whatever fits your classroom. The list can be expanded as students identify things they would like to know about each poet or poem. Jump-starter questions such as, "What did you notice about that poem?" or "Did you notice anything unusual about that poem?" are good places to start with any age. "How did that poem make you feel?" or "What do you think the poet who wrote that was feeling or thinking?" or "Does anyone know what made Emily Dickenson write that poem?" are also good ways to warm your students up to begin discussion.

If students seem uninterested or do not notice anything about the poem, you can either read it to them again, have one of them read it to the class, or ask the class why they think you find it interesting, pleasing, or displeasing. Then ask students, "What do you like and dislike about the poem?" Continue the discussion by prompting students with leading questions about content or style: "Did you notice any colors mentioned in that poem?" "What were the rhymes in that poem?" "Did that poem sound like someone talking normally or like someone singing?" "When do people speak in loud repetition like that?" "So what is the feeling of that poem?" "Do you think it was the poet who had that feeling or is it just the character in the poem?"

Any biographical data about the authors or facts about the making of their poems help actualize poetry as an art and as an internationally respected occupation. You might find yourself quoting interesting facts to your class that can augment other studies: "Walt Whitman wrote that poem while crossing the Delaware River. What other famous person is known for having crossed the Delaware? Langston Hughes wrote that famous poem while crossing which river? Listen to the poem again . . . . What famous explorers have we studied who crossed that same river?"

One question I am asked frequently by elementary students is, "Where do poets get ideas for poems?" I explain that poem ideas come from either the head, the heart, or the belly. This triad is something that children can grasp and instinctively relate to. Ask what type of poems come from the mind or head. Discuss the concept of "heartfelt" poems and songs. Ask if anyone has ever had a "gut feeling" and what emotions are related to the stomach (fear, fury, humor, hunger, joy, love, pain). These can become regular criteria in your poetry discussions: "Was that a head, heart, or belly poem?"

Note the effect that different types of poems have on your students. Some will comment on the meaning, mood, and content. Others will be swept up in the rhythm and style. One shy third grader showed her responses with smiles of joy or embarrassment or with frowns of perplexity or empathic sadness.

Let the poems do the work for you. Let students learn through their own poetry. We can only partially interpret a model poem for students. They will experience it in ways that are as unique as their own writings. A child may have a moment of epiphany upon hearing a classic poem. We can affirm children's responses by giving them language and asking them questions.

Often poems loosen feelings that a child has been waiting to talk about. Good poetry often contains symbols that touch each of us differently but profoundly. I have seen previously silent students cry or laugh out loud about writing on a certain topic. Open discussion of poems gives students word tools to control and express feelings. Everyone's response to a poem will be personal and, as with stories, based on feelings. Validating students' emotional responses to a poem quickens and deepens their willingness to try their own words in writing poems. A unique bond can form in the classroom through repeated formal discussion. Students know they can experiment with modes of expression rather than feeling pressured into emulating one manner of speech.

## USING IMPROVISED DISCUSSION AND IMPROMPTU WRITING ASSIGNMENTS

Sometimes an idea for a writing assignment will occur to you as the result of a discussion of current events, weather, important issues in the classroom, or someone's personal observation. If this happens, be prepared to improvise. Some of the best poems are written extemporaneously or are revised from impromptu journal entries. A writing assignment about something unexpected can succeed if the issue or idea has affected the whole class. A child can gain a great sense of meaning and purpose if, after making a unique, first-time observation, he or she creates a response that gains adult approval.

When children come to class laughing, crying, or arguing profusely about something, have a discussion about it. If a student's tale of a difficult incident on the street or excitement about a new baby sibling has already started a heated discussion, build on it. The student-centered discussion may delve into a subject deeply enough to warrant a writing assignment. You may not know of a structured writing assignment yet, but you can at least start prewriting and list-making of notes that will be used in a poem.

A prewriting discussion may cause an emotional issue to emerge that should be kept private or referred to parents. If you have taken note of such an issue and it surfaces again, you may find a writing exercise in this book or another curriculum resource that can suggest a way of dealing with it creatively or through the arts.

One group of students had been fighting on the playground and were told they now had to take recess inside. I asked half of the class to begin a poem about what the playground would be like without them, and the other half to write about what they would be like without the playground. A child who witnesses a butterfly emerge from a cocoon or sees a dog hit by a car on the way to school will benefit from writing about it, if only in a journal entry.

Some of my favorite classes just "happened" when I walked in and before saying a poem asked, "How are YOU? What happened over the weekend? What is going on in YOUR lives that is important?" As with all impromptu responses, you will know intuitively how far from your planned lesson a spontaneously generated topic deserves to go.

In most cases you can steer the discussion back toward your intended study area. When you are trying to encourage interest in a new topic or inspire a group to do something creative, formal discussion of an exemplary poem or equivalent prewriting experience is always helpful.

Both planned and impromptu dialogue about a piece of literature represents a chance to reflect on one's own experience with writing and creativity. And discussion can lift the veils of obscurity covering some poetry. Of those whom I have asked about their personal experience with writing in grade school, many say it was painful. And most of those people suggest that it was the pain of writing, not the obscurities of poetry, that turned them away from the art. The dialogue part of the writing process gives each of us, as instructors, the challenge of making writing meaningful and fulfilling to our students.

Finally, toward making the transition to writing their own poems, you may want to ask students questions like these, "Would you like to try writing something like that model poem?" "Let's try to write our own haiku poem about rabbits since we all miss Checkers!" "Can anyone tell me the haiku rules again?"

## BRAINSTORMING AND PREWRITING

After a discussion of what you are going to write about and before you assign solo writing, it helps students to go through the motions of creating a sample poem together. Without relevant topics and discussion, we are asking students to create poems from what is for them completely meaningless thematic subject matter. "If the teacher helps his pupils to enrich, quicken, and organize their material before they begin to write," said Rollo Walter Brown, "he not only stimulates them to their best efforts, but saves himself infinite pains."[4] Do a sample poem together on the chalkboard. It helps students to hear concrete examples of sometimes esoteric concepts, and to see a sample poem quickly appear. Still in a question-and-answer format with students, you can ask them for examples. Brainstorm images, lists, short examples, and group test poems in which each student contributes a part. In the upper grades, a student scribe with good handwriting can write these on the board while you ask questions and focus participation.

For example, if you are having students write a four-stanza science poem dealing with the concept of evaporation, and you have asked for similes about steam for each season, do a sample poem on the board about summer steam:

> "Who can tell me where one sees steam during the summer? Everyone shut your eyes and picture steam moving."
>
> Ice cream in the freezer! A street after it rains!
>
> "O.K., keep the street image for your own poem. For the group poem we'll use the freezer idea. What does the steam do?"
>
> Run down.
>
> "Run like what?"
>
> Like a white cat.
>
> "Yes, but how does it run?"
>
> It leaps.
>
> "So, is the steam *like* a cat or *is* it a cat?"
>
> It *is* a cat!
>
> "What type of leaping white cat?"
>
> A hungry one.
>
> "What was it doing in the freezer?"
>
> Eating ice cream.
>
> "Why does it run out?"
>
> Because it got caught with cold ice cream on its nose.

"Yes, of course it was cold and should never have been in the freezer.

"How about this: *Summer steam is a hungry white cat leaping out of the freezer like snow with legs*. Are there any changes anyone would like to suggest? Now try writing your own simile or metaphor with another season. Start your first one with, 'Autumn steam is . . . . ' and then go on from there. Raise your hand if you have any questions."

Writing a group poem on the board from student suggestions is also an opportunity for you to show poetry-editing skills in action. If you are the scribe, you can cross out or quickly erase suggestions that don't work, ask students for better suggestions, and add these to the list. This visually exhibits to the class the critical questioning, revising, and editing process.

Have the class read back the new sample poem together. Ask if there are any questions. Reexplain the expectations for individual writing and cite examples from the group poem. Ask if a couple of students can repeat the directions for the class.

Depending on the exercise, an individual student may benefit from more brainstorming, either with the student next to him or in a small group. Tell students how many minutes they have to write. List poems and parallel poems will benefit from the pressure of frenzied writing, but for most assignments, tell the students to take the time to think things through for themselves.

The prewriting brainstorm sessions are not just a way to mine raw material for poetry production. This phase of the writing process also gives students a chance to practice visualization and internal dialogue. Take the time to allow students to picture the scenes or images you want words for. Ask them to hear the words inside, to say them silently first. Does this or that phrasing sound better? Here, the left- and the right-handed, the visual and the verbal, the rational and the emotive, the linear and nonlinear student can meet, exchange, and try out ideas on the level playing field of poetry.

## ASSIGNING THE POEM

Give clear instructions for the writing assignment. Explain the type of interaction you want to have during the exercise. Make sure that students know when the mood and expectations change from receptive to responsive, from listening and watching to answering questions to writing to speaking and back to listening.

Always be prepared to handle exceptions. If a child understands the concept but begins to write a song instead of a poem, don't discourage it. If you see the child repeatedly using the same form and writing the same interpretations or themes, begin to make suggestions that he or she expand the repertoire.

Consider the alternative assignments that are attached to the bottom of each step-by-step writing exercise. If students proliferate in one area, these additional exercises are there to encourage and expand on student effort.

## WRITING A FIRST DRAFT

First drafts are exciting moments of creation when the mind of the student is churning out new ideas. While the writing is going on, make yourself available for suggestions and comments. Some students want to make sure they are going in the right direction. Others will covet and hide their creations until they feel they have something that is presentable. And as soon as they are finished with a poem draft, they will usually demand that you review their new creations.

In one class, I had to leave just when students were finishing writing. Excitement had reached such a peak that some students who had finished ran after me and threw their poems over the railing of the stairwell for me to catch. The desire for teacher recognition can be transformed into continued interest by announcing plans for the next poetry workshop.

Make it clear at the beginning of the writing time that when students feel they have finished with a draft, they can begin, on their own, to look over spelling, word choice, or things they would like to fix. You may already have devised a Self-Questioning Guide Sheet that your students use to check their work in other reading and writing areas. This can be a sheet of paper or a card that is kept inside their poetry folder. It can be mounted in the Poetree House. The Guide Sheet might contain a simple reminder list of editorial items that students can look for, such as spelling, word choice, line breaks, images, descriptions, sounds, colors, title, beginning, middle, end, name, date, and room number.

Then they can practice reading through the draft in order to become familiar with the rhythm, movement, and emphases of the poems. After checking through their Guide Sheets ask students to read their poems "aloud silently." By turning on their "inner voice" they can hear inside how it will sound when they read the poem out loud for the class.

Praise first drafts no matter what: "That's the right idea. Now see if you can add more images." "I like that." "That's a good poem. I like the part where . . . Let me make a suggestion." If the first draft isn't substantive enough to revise, don't. Have the student write another first-draft poem. But always have students read aloud what they've written, even if it is only one sentence. This is the sharing part of the poem-making process that builds character and community and excitement.

## STUDENT POETRY READING

Make this part as in depth as your class structure will allow. Some of you will have classrooms where verbal feedback from fellow students works well. Others will find it more productive to give each student a chance to read his or her work, and keep peer commentary to a minimum. Students can be asked to stand at their desks or stand in front of the class and to read their work loudly and clearly.

The experience of standing in front of the class with your heart on your sleeve can be daunting. Students can be asked to read their work gradually, as poetry becomes a more common part of your classroom. Teachers can stand next to or even touch the reader both for emotional and physical support, and for reading and pronunciation help.

Prefacing a poem with a brief explanation or an introduction is common. However, remind readers not to apologize for the poem that they are going to read, no matter how rough the draft. Emphasize the importance of taking a lot of deep breaths, standing up straight, introducing the poem, using a loud voice, and reading clearly. Some classes have the students read each poem twice. Some build equal participation by having everyone read first lines or favorite lines.

Have student readers thank the class for listening. At the end of each student's reading, some classes give a round of applause, and, with the teacher guiding the level of feedback, most shy students overcome their stage fright early in the year. If an atmosphere of mutual respect and support is developed in the classroom, students will enjoy reading and will write more as a result.

Reading aloud is a critical moment of self-discovery and learning. The very act of saying one's poems to an audience is one of confidence and pride. To externalize personal creativity and be praised is a fundamental building block of self-esteem. And the acquired ability to respond constructively to listener reaction can further develop one's sense of personal security, social responsibility, and citizenship.

Go to any open poetry reading in your area and you will see adults on stage exhibiting the same range of rooster-like self-confidence and paper-shivering nervousness that you have in your own classroom. After they step back down to earth and receive the usual "Good reading" and "Nice poem" praise, watch which ones seek out critical feedback.

The writing workshop critique sessions in each of these chapters are microcosms of social feedback for the individual. This need not be a negative experience. It can be experienced as supportive, encouraging, and instructive. The young workshop participant can be reminded that the feedback is about his or her writing, not his or her identity. I notice that both the shy and the show-off students exhibit their fears when they stand in front of the class to read their poems, especially when reading them for the first time. You can help by standing next to or behind them when they read. They just need to know they're not alone up there. You will notice even the cockiest students looking at you for your reaction immediately after they read their work.

It is important to have students present memorized poems repeatedly so that they can watch the reactions of the audience as they recite. This is a great source of personal empowerment. The best way that I have found to memorize poetry is to read the piece aloud to oneself or to an audience over and over again. Gradually, you will be able to look away from the text, and the words will still be there speaking to you from the page of your mind. If students are praised and rewarded, they will continue. But this is also a good place to begin the important work of critical thinking. If students learn the positive value of critique and evaluation and see repeated examples of their own work improving as a result of community feedback, this increases their desire for more experiences that can give them the same sensation.

## REVISING AND EDITING

Poems can be sent home as homework to be revised and edited with parents. Or you may have an open revision poetry session in class where students can work on the poem or writing of their choice.

Those students who feel tense about writing ideas or feel frustrated that perfection eluded them on the first try may show great excitement at revision time. Students can add to unfinished work, cut out lines, clean up poor endings, come up with better titles, and see their poems take shape.

## USING PEER CRITIQUE

Once students have finished revisions of poems in their folders, you can occasionally have a reading in which students present their favorite poems to the class and receive peer feedback. You should read yours as well. Your participation as instructor, fellow poet, and senior editor of the poetry workshops affirms student belief in the importance of writing.

Peer feedback can take place by having a reading in which classmates can raise their hands if they have suggestions for improvement. The Self-Questioning Guide Sheet and the Poetry Critique Guide Sheet can be used to frame comments about poems. Explain that comments should be made about the poems and not about the people who wrote them, and that this critique is meant to be constructive and helpful.

A written peer critique can be assigned during a class period. One copy of each student's poem can be passed out randomly with anonymous numbers on them so that when you collect them you can return them to their authors. Again, the Guide Sheets can be used. Also have readers circle the thing they like best and least about each poem. In the margins or on the back they can write what the poems mean to them and suggestions for improvements. Have these readers return poems to you in the same class session so that poems can be immediately filed in the authors' process portfolios.

Palmer, Hafner, and Sharp noted that a successful peer writing project was undertaken by a reading specialist at Casa de Oro Elementary School in Spring Valley, California. There, second-grade students who had just finished reading and discussing "Cinderella" wrote letters to characters in the story that expressed their unanswered questions. "Once the letters were written, revised, and edited," the study reported, "they were sent to the fifth grade class for answers."[5] In groups, fifth graders drafted, revised, and edited letters of response, which were then sent back to the second graders. Both classes benefited from one writing project.

## WRITING A FINAL DRAFT

With the suggestions of their peers, combined with their own edits, students can make final drafts that are pieces of art. This is the stage of poetry at which one can *abandon* a poem, according to the South African poet Dennis Brutus. There are many metaphors for the releasing of a piece of art into the world for public consumption. The point is that one can no longer edit it, play with it, change it, or recall it. Its beauty lies partly in the fact that it was created at a specific time in one's life. Send students to the word processor, typewriter, or paper at this stage and have them print out or photocopy three clean copies: one for their portfolios, one for your student record files, and one for their parents. If this can't happen at school, find parents who are able to type up poems once a month.

## PEER REVIEW POETRY READING

Have an occasional Best-of . . . reading where students can present their favorite finished poems. Ask listeners if they notice any changes from the rough draft, and what they think of the revised poems. Sometimes the raw and awkward elements of the rough draft poem will be what students remember and like about a poem.

During this reading you can quiz the students as to what type of poem is being read. Who knows what tools are being used in a particular poem? Does the poem persuade, inform, or describe? You can make final comments on writings and suggestions about the poet's reading style. Have students use their Guide Sheets to ask questions of fellow poets.

Record these readings on video or on audio cassette tape. The benefits to students who can see and hear themselves in action are incalculable. Students see the flaws and graces of their voices and movements in the mirror of technology and automatically make adjustments. It also nourishes their self-esteem to see and hear the fruits of their creative and intellectual labors immortalized for posterity. A separate audio tape for each child, though expensive, would be a valuable contribution to their Process Portfolios.

## EVALUATION AND ASSESSMENT

At this point the young writers have already received your comments and critique, as well as the verbal or written critiques of fellow students, and audience response. After a few poetry exercises, they should have a pretty clear sense of what they have been doing and what they like and don't like about poetry. Many of them will have begun writing poems on their own. They should also have an expanding vocabulary of evaluation words that they can use on poems, stories, articles, and other writing. Now each writer can evaluate his or her own success in poetry.

Have students conduct this evaluation at the end of the first and second report card period as part of the collection of poems for the anthology. Tell them that an editor will select work from submissions for an anthology, but that in this case students will make their own selections of poems they want to represent themselves. Ask them to write an accompanying explanation of why they chose their poems, what they learned from writing them, and what their goals are. You can decide whether the last question should relate specifically to writing or to the students in general. Perhaps these essays could appear with the poems.

A biographical sketch poem (use one of the several "I Am" poem exercises) should also be included in a student's portfolio. You can use this if you choose to publish student biographies in the back of the anthology.

You may want to precede this last assignment with a short individual meeting with the students in which you ask them to answer some verbal questions about the semester's poetry studies. You might focus on the grammatical mechanics learned through poetry, or on the content and what study areas students have included in their creative writing. The questions can be quiz-oriented or can occur in a discussion.

Drafts of poems should remain in portfolios to show how students' thought and writing skills change over a long period of time.

Evaluation and assessment at the end of the semester are made easier if students' folders are updated and assessed every few weeks. Some students will lose their Tool Box sheets. Some will lose poems when they take them home for editing. Set a schedule for photocopying your students' poems throughout the semester or year. This helps a great deal when and if you assemble an anthology of the students' best work at the end.

## DISPLAY, PUBLICATION, AND EXTRACURRICULAR APPLICATIONS

Several display ideas are explained in the Arts and Music chapter. Publication is also important. Children find it reaffirming to see their names in print and their poems published in a magazine or newspaper. This should happen repeatedly. At the end of the year an anthology of the students' best work can be published. With enough planning, a school budget can usually afford 50 copies of a 30-page anthology including 30 poems on 8½″ × 11″ paper, stapled or with a taped binding, and using only photocopied images. Your school's PTA or PTO may have a strategy for raising the money. If you include several classes, use high-quality graphics or photos, and make more copies, the price will be higher. Early planning is a good idea.

Computer class is a great place for students to print out their poems in various visual arrangements. If students can keep their poems on a computer disk or hard drive, they can easily edit them and print them out for publication.

Many publications are listed in the *Directory of Literary Magazines*,[6] which is published annually by the Council of Literary Magazines and Presses. Local newspapers, evening news shows, and radio stations also love doing stories on poetry classes, especially when a public reading is scheduled.

Readings can be organized at the school, the local library, or the local community center. Any place that has a microphone and an elevated stage works wonderfully. As with the classroom readings, it is very important to have a supportive teacher standing on stage for students to lean on when frightened.

Local literary and arts organizations usually have school adoption programs through which they will give your school special rates for attending readings by nationally known poets and writers or will even send writers to your school for a workshop or series of workshops. State arts councils have poet-in-residence programs in urban and rural areas that supply seasoned poets to help you conduct writing workshops.

Students who are at risk of failure for any reason can benefit from a visiting poet, or from watching a poet, playwright, or storyteller in a venue away from the school. The poets can become role models and mentors for students.

Parents can help with homework. They can also help in the classroom with editing and writing suggestions during the workshops and by reading poems to the class. Hearing a variety of adult voices and styles of presenting helps students develop their own voices and writing styles.

Take advantage of all the resources available to you and your students.

## NOTES

1. Peter Kelso, "Poems," in Richard Lewis, ed., *Miracles: Poems by Children of the English-Speaking World* (New York: Simon & Schuster, 1966), p. 15.

2. Alice Miller, *Prisoners of Childhood* (New York: Basic Books, 1987), p. 97.

3. Paulo Freire, *Pedagogy of the Oppressed* (New York: Seabury Press, 1970), p. 67.

4. Rollo Walter Brown, *How the French Boy Learns to Write* (Cambridge, MA: Harvard University Press, 1915).

5. Barbara C. Palmer, Mary L. Hafner, and Marilyn F. Sharp, *Developing Cultural Literacy through the Writing Process: Empowering All Learners* (Boston: Allyn and Bacon, 1994), p. 137.

6. Council of Literary Magazines and Presses, *Directory of Literary Magazines* (Wakefield, RI: Moyer Bell Limited, 1994).

# ▶ 2

# Art

This chapter contains exercises for writing poems about art, mixing visual with written art, and presenting poetry through visual arts and crafts. It also discusses other ways to record and display poetry. Some of the entries in this chapter are not writing assignments but activities you may refer to upon completion of written poems. As with the other arts, public presentation is an enjoyable and essential way to take poetry across the curriculum. The following activities offer ways to display poems, to encourage writing, and to understand other arts.

The poetry process portfolio, as suggested in this chapter, is a personalized way of storing poems written during the school year. The portfolio can work as an active anthology of a student's collected works. This is a good form of academic documentation because the writing of these poems can show a student's preparedness for creative use and articulation of his or her comprehension of a given study area.

Part of what inspires students to keep writing is the relief, surprise, and confidence inspired by the sudden appearance of a critical mass of their own work. If one day you notice that you have written a hundred poems, it is doubtful that you will ever stop writing.

*"Art is the center of the real world."*—Marcel Duchamp

## GIVE ME BEAUTY POEMS

Grades: 3–6

At every level of art study in the elementary grades, it is an important part of the curriculum for students to "be aware of beauty in art, in nature, and in their surroundings," according to one public school system's Instructional Planning Guides.[1] Beauty is, of course, in the eye of the beholder. Or, as the poet Baudelaire put it: "Beauty is for those who only see. Real beauty is for those who feel." But there are some forms of beauty on which you can probably get the whole class to agree.

**1.** Start with a few things you think are beautiful, but begin by using the figurative phrasing, "Beauty is . . ." or "Beauty is when . . ." If you write, for example, "Beauty is when the sun sets," have the class tell you what in particular makes or gives the sunset its beauty. This way, each stanza should have two beautiful lines.

> Beauty is when the sun sets,
> propping up its tired red feet and arms on the horizon.

**2.** With the older students, you may be able to make a more complex sentence. Focus on the source of the element of beauty. Ask them to help you write lines that say what "gives" the sunset its beauty, and from where it "takes" its beauty. Who or what "offers" it, and to whom or what does it "give" its beauty? These can be parallel poems (where repeating lines link with each other), prayer poems (where the giver of beauty is thanked or asked for more by the receiver), or simple list poems.

> Sunset gets its beauty from the clouds,
> and from sea where its bruised arms fish all day.
> Sea clouds offer sunset beauty in exchange for night.
> Sunset agrees and gives sea clouds night.
> Night is happy getting beauty from moon because
> moon takes beauty like candy from a baby sunrise.
> Sea gets beauty, by the way, from time and luck.
> It is happy to give it away before
> time and luck take it back. Gifted and wealthy
> but jealous of luck, time offers it nothing.
> Luck turns away, beauty scorned, waiting for sunset.
>
> —Aaren Yeatts Perry

## SPONGE BROADSIDE ACTIVITY

Grades: 1–6

A *broadside* is a kind of poetry poster—a one-page book. The broadside contains a single poem that is good enough to publish on its own, usually with fancy print and a background image or fancy border.

**1.** Make very faint pencil lines with a ruler where you want the lines of the poem to appear. Regular bond typing paper will work fine, but there are many different papers that will also work. Papers that allow liquid to bleed or run, such as newsprint, construction paper, and onionskin, will not work unless bleeding is an artistic technique you want to employ.

**2.** Write the poem in calligraphy, with stencils, or with unique handwriting, centered in the middle of the page. A computer printout with an unusual font in a slightly larger-than-usual point size will work also. I suggest the hand-made effect of using wax or oil crayons, but indelible or regular ink will work fine.

**3.** After writing the poem on the page, apply with a sponge or wadded-up rag any color of tempera paint or water color. Make sure the paint is somewhat diluted. If you are using a heavier paint mixture or a darker color, apply the color first. Then write the poem over the pattern you have made.

**4.** Experiment with the size, shape, and texture of the sponge, and with the shade of ink or paint. Sponges can be cut out in the shapes of plants and animals. Items from science units such as shells and rocks also may be used to apply the colored paint over the poem.

## MASK POEMS AND ACTIVITY

Grades: 1–6

Cross-curricula: Social Studies

Preactivity Class Reading: Dudley Randall's "A Different Image"[2] and Paul Lawrence Dunbar's "We Wear the Mask"[3]

After doing any mask-making activity, whether with paper or with plaster gauze, students can write poems to go along with their masks. They can be displayed either next to or *on* the masks!

Younger students can help you write a compare-and-contrast group poem about what the mask shows and what it is hiding. If you make animal masks, for example, the poem can be a stanza of two to six couplets saying what the mask shows about the animal beneath. The students can come up with descriptive words about the mask character, its special powers and wishes. What can your mask character do that you can't do?

Older students can create a metaphor for the mask by brainstorming a list of qualities that indicate someone who is introverted or hiding something: shyness, quietness, embarrassment, sneaking, shame, dramatic smile, "blackface" (as in, "puttin' on the cork" or "burnt cork" in Randall's poem), guilt, secret knowledge. This can be a persona poem in which students use metaphors to describe who they are while in the masks. Ask them to identify five to ten things that the mask turns them into.

Another approach for students is to imitate the Randall poem where the task is to "reanimate the mask," and write a "Used to Be/But Now" poem. The poem can say what they used to be without the mask and who they are now that they are wearing it.

You can have them memorize these poems to say while wearing the masks or have them memorize the dramatic Dunbar piece to recite as a group while wearing masks.

*"What's the face you had before you were born?"*—Zen Koan

## BODY-TRACING ACTIVITY

Grades: All

Body tracing is a great way for students to display their poems, become conscious of their stage of development, and compare their shapes with those of other kids. I have helped trace and cut out the shapes of children from toddlers to high school seniors. For poetry, at least two different types of cutouts can work.

A full-body cutout can be made simply by tracing around the student, or having students trace each other on a roll of brown butcher paper. The poses, the decorations, and the poems written in them are chosen by the student. These cutouts should contain some of the student's best poems to put on display. This is a great way to display any of the body poems from the Health chapter (Chapter 4).

Another suggested cutout shape for displaying poetry is the bust of the student—that is, the body from the torso up. Bust cutouts take up less room on the wall when displayed. A "thought bubble" can emerge from the mouth of the poet with his or her poem written inside it.

A variation on this is a rainbow bust. Here, a student's short poem is written inside a rainbow. The student's hands are held out to either side of her body as if holding something. The rainbow arcs over her head, extending from hand to hand. This requires a careful cutting job. The image or images and all decorative work should be complete before you cut the paper.

If you don't want students lying on the floor to be traced, you can use a slide projector. Have each student in turn simply stand in front of the projector light to cast a shadow on a sheet of paper that has been taped onto the wall. The shadow can be reshaped until satisfactory and then quickly traced while the model holds still.

## DIAMANTE KITE POEMS

Grades: 3–6

Cross-curricula: Science

This form works well for any compare-and-contrast poem exercise in which opposites are compared. It can be used as a title poem like those suggested in the Personalized Poetry Process Portfolios activity at the end of this chapter. These poems can use any of the content themes in this book.

**1.** Tell students that they are going to write a poem called a *diamante*. Ask if anyone knows what the word means (it's Spanish for "diamond") or can guess what shape the poem makes. Draw the diamond shape on the board. Show a picture of a diamond and explain how similar it is to the shape of a regular four-sided kite.

**2.** Pass out sheets of paper with the diamante instructions on one side and the simple shape of a kite, with tail and string, on the other side. Leave space on the rules side for students to write their rough drafts. Explain that when the poem is finished, a revised version can be written in the diamond-shaped kite on the other side. As you are circulating, ask students to list other things that are shaped like a diamond. Crystals, snow cones, and kites are comparable in shape.

**3.** Write a group diamante on the board with the students. Use some opposites and facts from your current science unit—for example, *star/planet, paper/wood, night/day, cold/hot, liquid/solid, coal/diamond.*

**4.** The diamante structure is as follows. The first line of the diamante poem contains one word: a noun that is the opposite of the last word. The second line contains two words: adjectives describing the first word. The third line consists of three *-ing* or *-ed* verbs about the subject in the first line. The fourth line has four words: nouns about the subject in the first and last lines. The fifth line contains three *-ing* or *-ed* verbs about the subject in the last line. The sixth line contains two words: adjectives describing the subject in the last line. The seventh line contains a one-word subject: a noun opposite the noun in the first line.

Finished diamante kite poems can be cut out and suspended from doorways, ceilings, or lighting fixtures individually or together in groups as mobiles.

Glass
Smooth, see-through
Shining, drinking, curving
Beach, terrarium, hour glass, castle
Flowing, blowing, shifting
Gritty, quick
Sand

The *cinquaine* poem is also shaped like an upside-down kite. If students show an interest, the same process described above can be assigned, but using the cinquaine form. The first line has two syllables (title). The second line has four syllables (description of title). The third line has six syllables (action). The fourth line has eight syllables (feeling). The fifth line has two syllables (summary or different word for the title).

Another type of kite that can display a poem in the classroom is the Chinese fish kite.

**1.** To make a fish kite, bend a piece of hanger metal into a rigid hoop. Be sure to tape any jagged ends. This circular opening is the mouth of the fish. It should be about eight inches in diameter; big enough so that five or more poem strips can be taped to each one.

**2.** Have students write their poems on one long strip of paper. The length will depend on the height of your ceilings or light fixtures. The longer the paper, the more visually stunning.

**3.** Decorate one end of the paper with the open mouth and eyes of a fish and attach to the round fish-mouth top of the kite. Decorate the rest of it with colorful fins, gills, and scales. These become the kite's streamers. Any type of poem can be used here if it can be written in one long line, using commas, colons, and slash marks to indicate line breaks. In the end, the suspended poem strips look like an octopus/squid or an eel/lamprey.

## POETRY LANTERNS AND CARDS ACTIVITY

Grades: 1–6

Cross-curricula: Social Studies

Preactivity Class Reading: *Festivals Together: A Guide to Multicultural Celebration*, by Fitzjohn, Weston, and Large[4]

Another easy arts-and-crafts poetry project is the lantern. Poetry can be written on the paper of either the paper bag lantern or the Chinese lantern so that the words of the poems glow. These display projects should be done only with adults present, as they involve candles.

### *Bag Lantern*

**1.** With the bag lantern, have students write their finished poems on small brown paper bags first. You can use bags of any size, but the lunch bag size is thin enough to be illuminated by a candle.

**2.** After you write poetry on one or all four sides, pour two inches of sand (or very small pebbles) into the bottom of the bag. A pencil or chopstick glued or taped to an inside corner (or all four inside corners) helps make the lantern rigid.

**3.** Place a small candle in the sand. To avoid burns, light the candle with a long fireplace match.

## Chinese Lanterns

Chinese lanterns are easy to make. Clear directions for constructing the body of the lantern can be found in *Festivals Together*. This book contains myths and stories that can be read to students in preparation for many cultural festivals.

The basic Chinese lantern can be cut out of a rectangular piece of stiff paper or cardboard. Try going through the motions with a regular piece of typing paper first.

**1.** Fold the paper longways so that the fold runs the length, not the width, of the paper. Cut wavy lines from the fold (perpendicular to the long edge) about three-quarters of the way across the paper. Write the lines of the poem in dark ink on the light-colored paper of the lantern slats or wavy cuts.

**2.** Now open the paper, wrap it into a cylinder, and glue the two short edges together. Staple or glue a doubled but narrow strip of paper (or a reed or husk) across the top for a handle.

**3.** Cut a circular piece of cardboard slightly smaller than the opening of the bottom, fold the bottom edges of the paper underneath the cardboard circle, and glue or tape it. A small candle can be placed in the middle of this circle and held in place by pushing a pin up through the bottom and into the candle.

**4.** To retain its shape and keep the muffin-shaped lantern from collapsing, poke two chopsticks up through the bottom of the cardboard and tape them to the top of the cylinder.

## Glow Cards

A greeting card can be made using the same principle of rear illumination.

**1.** Write a very short poem on a piece of onionskin, rice paper, or very lightweight typing paper in colored or dark ink.

**2.** Cut a square or rectangle a little larger than the size of the poem out of the front of a folded greeting card that is rigid enough to stand up by itself. Cut the poem out of the paper. Leave enough excess paper to glue to the inside of the standing greeting card.

**3.** Decorate the front of the card around the poem. When a small candle is placed behind the card, the letters of the poem will stand out on the glowing paper.

## COLORS

Grades: 1–6

Cross-curricula: Science, English, Music

Color is a universal theme in writing poetry; it can be a subject unto itself or a doorway to better description. The mental image of a color and the sounds of color names can be very evocative in poetry. Verbal images like color names can help in completing the pictures that are the hallmark of good poetic imagery. This section suggests several different color-related writing exercises.

### *Color Acrostics*

Write the name of any color vertically down the left side of the page. This is the quickest way to get students to begin making relationships between a color and its associated images and objects. Colors with longer names or compound colors can provide more letters for older students. Each letter can begin a phrase or a sentence about what the color means to the poet, objects known to be that color, wishes, desires, concerns, or lies told by that color if it could talk.

### *Compound Colors*

Imagine that there are three thousand shades of every color. To produce a list of compound colors, ask students where or on what objects they see, for example, yellow. Phone book yellow becomes a color. So does stop light or yield sign yellow, lemon yellow, bicycle yellow, meringue yellow, silk scarf yellow. When or where do students see the color orange? Pumpkin glow under darknight sky orange.

*Colors*

Turquoise
Raspberry
Bittersweet
I love when we really eat.
Royal Purple
Fuschia
Marblue
I like those colors too.

Jungle green
Marigold
Cerulean blue
Do you like those colors too?

—Tiffany Bosely (Grade 5)

## *Color Similes and Metaphors*

While colors are good tools for describing objects, and objects can describe color, similes and metaphors can also help in deepening description. Discuss the concept of similes. Create a few simple comparisons on the board using your favorite color with both *like* and *as.* Ask the class for some similes to describe some of their favorite colors. When you have completed the group list, have students write their own list of simile comparisons. After reading some of these out loud together, ask students to look at the metaphors that emerge when they rewrite the list changing *like* or *as* to *is.*

## *Biography of Colors*

**1.** Brainstorm a list of facts that you would like to know about each color. The answers will be fabricated by the poets.

**2.** Model a group version on the board. Blue was invented by . . . Blue is now owned by . . . In its spare time blue . . . At midnight, blue . . . The worst thing that happened to blue . . . If you wake up blue . . . Blue likes to eat . . . One of blue's best kept secrets is . . . Blue says . . . Blue used to be . . . What I like about blue is . . . Blue is my friend because once . . . When blue meets yellow and red they all . . .

**3.** After reading the group poem together, assign each student to write about one color or one of the compound colors the class has invented.

Similar story poems can be written about "How the Colors Invented Themselves." The first verse of "America the Beautiful" has excellent use of color. Write it on the board to let students see the phrasing. Then students can write a color anthem poem describing the beautiful colors of their own neighborhood, home, school, state, planet, or recent science or social studies content.

## *Color Memories*

**1.** Discuss color memory. Start with who in the classroom is wearing certain colors. Ask students to look at the color they are wearing. Ask if anyone has a memory that is attached to that color.

**2.** Write a few of the examples on the board. Red reminds me of . . . Yellow makes me feel safe the way it did when . . . I remember . . . when I see this color of brown. Similes and metaphors are good ways of describing memories also: "Yellow scares me/like when I got lost/in the store." "My grandmother in the hospital/silver all around her bed/like pearls and bracelets, silver tears flowing into silver hair, silver dream."

In revision, students can be asked to specify the exact color and deepen their descriptions of memories.

**3.** Have each student write a line of memory about each color they are wearing.

## WORD PICTURE POEMS

Grades: 2–4

Word pictures can take the place of visual pictures. In this exercise, your students can enter their pictures through words. All students should have large pictures that they have painted or colored. Multiple images are helpful but not necessary. This activity can work even if the picture contains a single image of a car, a flower, or an animal, or even an abstract scribble.

**1.** Draw a simple figurative scene on the board—a picture of a house with a chimney next to a tree with a sun and a dog in some grass. Ask students for the words that go with each image.

**2.** Once the words are in the same places as the images were, ask a student to read the word pictures. Boring? Exactly. "House dog tree sun boy sit bat grass," seems oversimplified. At best it may be a good "found poem." But it is really a prewriting exercise leading toward more descriptive word pictures.

**3.** Ask the class for better descriptions, more poetic words that fit their own interpretations of the story in the picture.

**4.** Once you have created a poetic story describing the picture and the class has read it, ask students to write their own poem-stories for pictures that they have drawn.

**5.** Have some of the students read their few-words pictures, and ask the listeners to tell what they saw from the words. Is what the listeners saw the same as what the author intended? Have the author show the original picture to the class.

**6.** Now have the author finish the picture by describing it further in words. For example, ask them questions about what is going on in the picture. Use colors, textures, shapes, similes, metaphors, and other descriptive words to fill out the objects in the picture. Use action: What has been happening, what just happened, what is about to happen? Why? Who else is there or not there? Use the Poetry Critique Guide Sheet to come up with questions, senses, and other useful poetry tools to fill out the word picture.

## PHOTOCOPY BROADSIDE POEMS AND ACTIVITY

Grades: 1–6

The same type of poetry display can be created with the help of a photocopier. If you can afford the film, it is fun to have each student take an instant photograph of something related to a specific study area. This photo can then be copied and enlarged, and the poem written on the copy. Objects relating to specific areas of study, as well as objects from home, also can be placed on the photocopier glass—with great caution! These images can be combined with poems (see values and science poems). Finally, the student's hand can be placed on the copier screen, and a poem can be written in the hand part (see fortune teller poems).

The finished product may be duplicated for the poet's family or for display in the school. For copyright reasons, photographs chosen for duplication should be only those that were taken by the family of the poet or by the poet himself.

If the photographs that you use for your photograph poems in this same section are over fifty years old or are for some other reason free of copyright restriction, these make wonderful broadsides, as the imagery and description in the poems are usually quite rich.

*"The purpose of art is to stop time."*—Bob Dylan

## PHOTOETRY: WHO'S WHO POEMS

Grades: 3-6

This is a writing exercise in which classmates write poems about each other's likenesses from photographs, without knowing who's who!

**1.** Ask students to bring in both a baby picture and a current picture of themselves. Tell students they will be comparing baby pictures with one another. Ask them to bring the pictures in a plastic bag so that they don't get damaged. If for some reason many students have no baby pictures, this activity can be done with current pictures. Have an instant camera handy on the day of the writing assignment for those who forget their pictures. Make sure that the name of the student is on the back of each photo.

**2.** First show the students some photographs of yourself as a child. Have the students help you write a group poem on the board about yourself.

**3.** As with the found poems, mix up the baby photos in a bag and have each student draw one. Make sure that no one gets his or her own photo, so that poems can be written about the baby pictures by someone other than the person in the photo. A good starting title might be, "What I Think You Should Know about Judy," "What You Might Not Know about Dan," or "What I Notice about Gerry."

**4.** These poems can compare the baby's cute looks to something, someone, an animal, or a type of food. Encourage students to write with authority, as if the poet had been present from the birth of the child he is writing about. Suggest that the poets create an endearing nickname for the baby. Try to have them pick out something positive and make a positive prediction about what it means—for example, "You can tell by her rainbow widow's peak that she one day will be a great . . ." or "I can see by the devil's pool of his dimples that he will one day be president." These rules and optional beginnings can be written on the board and then reiterated as you circulate around the room during the solo writing.

**5.** Have the students read their poems aloud before revealing who each one is. See if classmates can guess which baby the poem is about.

**6.** For the second writing, have the poets write about themselves, looking at both the baby picture and the current picture. This can be an "I Used to Be/But Now I Am" poem or an "I've Changed from X to Y" poem. It can be written by students about themselves, but in the third person, as a "Something about Juanita" poem. That is, each line can begin with, "There's something about Juanita, the way she dresses reminds me of . . . looks like . . . makes you say . . ." "The Really Beautiful Extra Awesome Unique and Special Something about Veronique" can have as many adjectives as it wants, but try to make the poem reveal the things to which those adjectives refer. Finally, the Acrostic poem is always a useful form to use in picking out and writing observations from photos.

The most important aspect of any one of these approaches is specificity of detail and description. The photo provides exact detail that a mental picture cannot.

**7.** Photos also stop time so that a hidden expression or identity may be revealed. And this concept provides us with another writing exercise or poem title: "If Time Stopped Here," or, "Stop Here, I Want to Get Off," in which the writer can list all the things they like about their particular age and muse upon what would happen if they stayed that age and if nothing changed.

## PHOTOETRY: CLOSE-UP POEMS

Grades: 3–5

Cross-curricula: Science

Preactivity Class Reading: Theodore Roethke's, "Moss-Gathering"[5]

**1.** Bring photographs of objects into the classroom. Using a large picture that everyone can see, write a group poem on the board. Describe it without naming it. Question the class about the smallest details of the object. Use phrases and single words. Ask for imaginative descriptions one cannot immediately discern from a photograph: smell, texture, sound, movement. Avoid describing the surrounding environment unless it helps you describe what the object is or what it does.

**2.** Then give students their own pictures to work from. These can be pictures from science class. Have them write close-up riddle poems about the object in the picture.

**3.** A riddle poem can be assigned. This type of poem describes everything about an object and its qualities without naming the object. A student looking at a picture of jelly could say: "My poem is made of gooey, sticky, bright red sweetness. It clings to toast like Elmer's glue. While it waits to get in my mouth it turns to Kool Aid. . . ."

**4.** As an alternative, have students tell of a memory (real or imagined) of when they discovered the object for the first time and were brought face to face with it (see Color Poems).

*The Hunter (Photograph Poem)*

Suddenly I'm walking inside a black hole
so dark and deep. Soon you will meet,
said a loud voice which I was curious
where it came from. Suddenly I feel
as if I'm falling. I'm no longer
in the hole. Arggh! I am transforming
into something but I can' take the pain.
The pain is gone but I look like an animal.
I have black spots. I start to hunt
not knowing what I am. I'm a
mountain lion.

—David Mendez (Grade 4)

## PHOTOETRY: CLOSER UP POEMS

Grades: 3–6

Cross-curricula: English, Science

Preactivity Class Reading: Theodore Roethke's "Moss-Gathering";[5] Walt Whitman's "Once I Pass'd through a Populous City"[6]

**1.** Bring in photographs or pictures of single objects depicted at very close range—little, simple things that usually don't command much importance. Some teachers bring boxes of objects that are displayed on a table or placed on student's desks individually. You can use moss, a shell, a rock, jelly, an egg, a clam, a hairpin, a bone, an oily rag, wood, a chain, a rose petal, various tools, and other safe objects identifiable or unidentifiable to children.

**2.** Begin by using one large picture. Display the large image of a detailed object in front of the classroom. Discuss its physical qualities, its unchanging and changing qualities. Draw out all the details and list them on the board.

**3.** Then give students their own images to work with. For a prewriting exercise, write as many details as possible. Then create a group poem on the board in which you use the details of the description as if the poem itself were made of the object. "This poem is sharp as a thorn on one end and straight as a tiny arrow. This poem holds my sister's hair up. She always loses this poem." These can be riddle poems in which the actual object is not named but described. Now have students create their own object poem.

**4.** Trade images. Add another stanza to this poem in which students write of their first memories of discovering or encountering their objects. (Memories, again, can provide a wellspring of creative juices in describing small things in photographic detail.)

**5.** Remembering in detail can also lead to poems of contrast. In the style of Walt Whitman's "Once I Pass'd through a Populous City," discuss a trip the class took together. Have them write a poem contrasting details of what they thought they would remember to what they did actually remember.

Students can concentrate on the details of an event that happened on the trip, or create a panoramic vision in which they describe many things using similes. "On our way to the Liberty Bell, cars rushed like the Indy 500, trash everywhere like a junkyard park . . ." "There were more babies in carriages than elephants, more popcorn and pigeons than eagles, more teachers than llamas . . ."

*"My writing is a picture of the mind moving."*
—Phillip Whalen

# FORTUNE TELLER BROADSIDE POEMS AND ACTIVITY

Grades: 1–6

**1.** Invite a palm reader or fortune teller into the classroom to read the students' palms. The visitor can explain the tradition to the class. If there are no corner fortune tellers in your area, consult a book on palmistry or chiromancy, the art of telling fortunes from the visual lines, marks, and patterns on the palm. Discuss the concept of foretelling the future. Explain the difference between scientific predictions made by astronomers and meteorologists, and those made by nonscientific fortune tellers using such things as yarrow sticks, I Ching coins, tarot cards, astrology charts, numerology, palmistry, and dream analysis (oneiromancy).

**2.** Fingerprints and handprints are swirling spirals of one-of-a-kind skin formations used by detectives and police forensics labs to identify who has touched what at a crime scene. Invite a lab technician or a detective into the classroom to fingerprint your own classroom as a "learning scene"! Have the visitor explain the phenomenon before you make the poetry-writing assignment.

**3.** As with the photographs, most parents will allow their children to bring a copy of their birth certificate with foot-, hand-, and fingerprints into the classroom. If these are not available in your class, you can use the old tempera paint handprint method. You can also use an ink pad to fingerprint your students. Black ink copies best. Footprints, ear prints, and lip prints have also been done—but only with parental permission, in a safe and clean environment, with water-soluble ink or paint, and with adequate clean-up supplies.

**4.** When you have either a finger- or handprint from each student, take the prints to a copy machine and enlarge them until they fill a sheet of paper. These can be used as a broadside picture background over which to write the following poem.

**5.** Students can read their own palms or fingerprints. Have them write a divination poem declaring that they can see into the future through the print. Write the names of the lines on the board: life line, family line, work line, and spirit line. For fingers, you can start in the center of each print and write, first finger line, second line, third line, etc. You may even ask students to look at their prints and then close their eyes or put their heads down before they tell "what they see."

**6.** This poem of instruction and authority can begin each line with soothsayer language: "I can see from my life line that . . ." "Looking at my hand I see . . ." "My work line shows me . . ." "My spirit line clearly takes me to . . ." Ask for places imagined and situations or even things, rather than amounts of money. Do they see any shapes in the lines?

**7.** If your class is one in which students can read each others' prints, put names on the back and pass out copies. Ask for specifics: "In the center of your fingerprint spiral, I see an inside-the-park home run in the third inning with men on first and third. In the second ring I can hear the crack of the bat. In the swirl there I see you sliding into home. I cannot tell if you are safe. In the fourth line where it curves like your cheekbones, I see the face of a dog chasing someone home from school. No. The dog is being chased. The dog has someone's poems in its mouth . . ."

**8.** A sixth grader may be able to write a found poem using the many dictionary entries under the word *palm*.

### *Fingerprint Haiku Card*

A haiku or renga poem with only the fingerprint as the signature will fit neatly on a greeting card for any occasion. This can be completed in one class session by handing out blank 3" × 5" cards or 5" × 7" cards on nicer stock. Students can place the poem and fingerprint in any arrangement on the card and write their name, the date, and an addressee on the other side. Or they can simply use an 8½" × 11" sheet of paper folded in half, and write a longer message on the inside. If you are working with grades 1 through 3, you may want to have the students copy down a group poem from the board to go with the fingerprint (see the section on Haiku Business Card poems).

## GROUP POEMS BOOK ACTIVITY

Grades: 2–6

Whenever you conduct a writing workshop where an outcome is a group poem, the Group Poems Display Book can be a wonderful way to document it. This is a book that can store any group poems written by the class and can be read from during public presentations.

**1.** Find a large photo album in a three-ring or multiring binder. It should be at least 11" × 17" in size. You will also need to find some continuous run computer spreadsheet printout paper. This paper is usually 11" × 17" and comes in cartons of hundreds of pages, each sheet connected to the next by a folded and perforated line.

**2.** Take any poem for which each student has written a line or stanza as part of a whole poem. Have students rewrite their own lines in sequence on the spreadsheet, with their initials on their page. Even if the line contributed by a student is only a few words long, it can still take up at least one 11" × 17" sheet.

**3.** The first page should be a title page. The second page should begin the poem. After the last line of the poem, you may want the book to include the authors' names on one page. Either the authors' page can be typed and inserted, or they can autograph the page themselves. The last page may have a dedication or explanation of the type of poem.

**4.** When the writing is complete, your class may want to turn the paper over carefully and draw, paint, or decorate in some manner the side that will face the audience. A sign can be created that reads, "Mrs. Modiglioni's Fourth-Grade Group Poem of the Year," so that, as the poem is being read by the students in sequence, the sign is unfurling to the audience.

**5.** Vertically secure the last 5 to 10 pages in the photo album binders by using a hole punch. This gives the paper a sturdy attachment. The accordion stack of paper should be placed so that when the album is opened, you can pull out the paper in a continuous sheet from the book to the left. This allows a poem to be read from left to right as one walks away from the book holding the leading edge or first sheet of the paper.

**6.** Once the pages are carefully folded back into the book and the cover of the book is titled, students can line up in the order in which their line or stanza appears in the poem. Each student reads his or her section and then slowly walks the paper away from the book. You can stand at the book itself to help them hold the book and read into a microphone. If you are doing this for an assembly, make sure the poem is no longer than the stage is wide. If you are doing it on the playground, make sure there is a megaphone at the book site and that the day is not too windy!

Once the poem is completely unfolded, the students should be standing in a line across the stage. At this point they can read the poem again in sequence from where they are standing.

I have found by trial and error that it is wise not to tear any of the perforated sheets while creating this poem. It takes quite a tape job to repair it properly. Tape can be applied as a safety precaution before writing in the book, at the outside edges of the paper near the folds.

*"Why shouldn't we give children the future? Isn't it theirs?"*
—James Dolsen

## THE POETRY PROCESS PORTFOLIO

Grades: All

Cross-curricula: All

Preactivity Class Reading: *A Teacher's Guide to Creating Portfolios* by Martin Kimeldorf[7]

A poetry process portfolio can be an enjoyable way for students and teachers to document the process used and the progress made in working together on poetry. A portfolio provides a body of material to critique, assess, evaluate, and compare with other evaluations. Most important for elementary students, it can be a place for recognition and reward. From infancy through adolescence, children need constant positive feedback. They need to know that they are pleasing themselves, their peers, and the power figures in their lives. It is partly from this sense of accomplishment that children can build the positive self-image that fuels achievement and success. Regular review of the portfolio is an important way of giving this feedback to all students.

Reward students by giving them more folders when the first one is filled up. Make sure that all drafts of a poem go into the folder so that students get in the habit of saving the writing rather than throwing anything out. Seeing edit marks and lines through words on imperfect drafts helps students recognize that writing is a process of exploration, full of trial and error. Equating drafts with success rather than failure helps build the self-esteem needed later in life to handle rejection letters from magazines, a critique from an editor, or a loss in a poetry contest. Also, if students throw out drafts that they don't like, they may also be throwing out drafts that they should like. If poems by students or their photographs appear in any publications, they should be kept in the portfolio.

The student Process Portfolio may also include documentation of clubs and activities, report cards, papers on science projects, collages, some expression of involvement with foreign language, peer tutoring documentation, and cassettes or videos of the student performing poetry. If the students in your classroom were adults doing as much work as the students do in a given school year, there would probably be a whole wall covered with filing cabinets, and at least one file drawer for each student. The process portfolio is a way of reminding students how much they accomplish in a given year. Will the elementary schools of the future provide these?

## PERSONALIZED POETRY PROCESS PORTFOLIOS

Grades: 1–6

Ideas abound about the best way to decorate a student's personal folio. My favorite is an "opposites" approach to titling and decorating it. From a child's first words, opposites are an important part of speech and communication. They make great titles, too: Black and White, Apples and Oranges, Night and Day, Dogs and Cats, Paper–Scissors–Rock, Light and Dark, Fast and Slow, Past and Present, Silence and Words, Half Empty and Half Full. These opposites can come from the students' favorite study units or from their own inside jokes or secret language. The titles of the poems included in the portfolio should be written on the inside cover, like a table of contents. Include the name of the student, the date, and classroom number on every draft. If a student's portfolio is overflowing, reward his proliferation with a new one. On the inside cover, a diamante poem (or any opposites or contrast poem) can be written using these two words.

The accordion book is another good form of publishing display. Collaborate with the art teacher and assemble an accordion book of any size. Glue together and fold back and forth as many pages of construction or typing paper as you need to give the poems a place to live. A pocket accordion book is something students can carry around and read from if the poems are written small enough. If you use construction paper, you can place such objects as shells, a beaded necklace, paper clips, or sticks on the cover and set them out in the sun to create a silhouette on the paper. The color and texture of the folder owned by the child will influence the possible colors of decorations. Some students use computer drawing and coloring to illustrate their poems.

Don't underestimate the importance of the form in which a poet's work is stored and made accessible. It is the beginning of lifelong work habits, the external expression of the internal rituals of the creative process. It is the child's press package, his résumé, his passport as a diplomat in the local and international arena of the arts. It can and should look attractive to the student.

## NOTES

1. School District of Philadelphia, *Instructional Planning Guides Grades 1–8* (Philadelphia: Board of Education, 1994).

2. Dudley Randall, "A Different Image," in Richard Ellmann and Robert O'Clair, eds., *The Norton Anthology of Modern Poetry* (New York: W. W. Norton, 1973), p. 868.

3. Paul Lawrence Dunbar, "We Wear the Mask," in Alexander W. Allison et al., eds., *The Norton Anthology of Poetry, Revised* (New York: W. W. Norton, 1975), p. 945.

4. Sue Fitzjohn, Minda Weston, and Judy Large, *Festivals Together: A Guide to Multicultural Celebration* (Gloucestershire, UK: Hawthorn Press, 1993).

5. Theodore Roethke, "Moss-Gathering," in Michael Spring, ed., *Where We Live: Scholastic American Literature Program* (New York: Scholastic Magazines, 1977), p. 27.

6. Walt Whitman, "Once I Pass'd through a Populous City," in Michael Spring, ed., *Where We Live: Scholastic American Literature Program* (New York: Scholastic Magazines, 1977), p. 72.

7. Martin Kimeldorf, *A Teacher's Guide to Creating Portfolios* (Minneapolis, MN: Free Spirit Publishing, 1994).

## RECOMMENDED READING

Michael Spring, ed., *Where We Live: Scholastic American Literature Program* (New York: Scholastic Magazines, 1977), pp. 212–213.

# ▶ 3

# English

Poetry, like song, can have universal appeal. It is written and spoken in hundreds of languages around the world. Poetry has been practiced by literate and preliterate societies from before recorded history. Through nursery rhymes poetry is sometimes the first speech a child repeats.

*This Is a Poem*

This is a poem about god looks after things:
He looks after lions, mooses and reindeer and tigers,
Anything that dies,
and mans and little girls when they get to be old,
and mothers he can look after,
and god can look after many old things.
That's why I do this.

—Hillary-Anne Farley (Age 5, Canada)[1]

In this chapter, elements of English grammar are infused into the writing exercises. Nouns, verbs, and adjectives, for example, become parts of thinking and writing games. Making a poem can help a student master English grammar skills by giving the student an opportunity to use a grammatical rule repeatedly with student-generated examples. Repeatedly writing and speaking new information in the classroom gives a student ownership and greater retention of language rules through the art-making process.

This section discusses the importance of keeping a journal, a basic practice for the development of language facility and application. Having a place to write brief journal entries, review poetry exercises, take notes, and write rough drafts can help secure a student's commitment to writing in general.

Some poetry forms are also included here as they relate to English literature. While many forms are not included, such as the Spanish-language *decima,* others are listed in the glossaries of this book. If students show more interest in writing in metered verse or any of the forms, let them continue and show them others.

## FIRE DRILLS

Grades: All

Cross-curricula: All

One method of doing what McKim and Steinbergh call fire drill poems[2] is to write a word on the board and have the students write down all the words that come to mind in one minute, or in a given time period.

A fire drill is a quick way to write a list poem. This is a great prewriting exercise that encourages free thinking and generative writing. Fire drills help get relevant words on paper so that they can be worked into a poem. Throughout all of the exercises that follow, it is important to remind young writers that the first thing they write probably won't be perfect. The objective is not perfect poetry, but learning the fun and importance of the poetry-writing process.

**1.** Choose a key word from a recent lesson. The word should have enough familiarity and relevance to the students that they will easily relate other words to it. The word itself should be visually evocative, like *Egypt* or *dental hygiene.*

**2.** Begin the group fire drill by writing the word in big letters on the chalkboard. Assign the job of timekeeper to one student.

**3.** Immediately have students raise their hands. Ask them to tell you the words that entered their thoughts when they saw the word you wrote. This will give you a list of words that you can use in many other poetry-writing exercises.

**4.** Have the students write this list of words in a vertical line down the page for their poetry folders. Then ask the students what type of poem they think they can write using these words. Can one of the students read the list backwards? Does reading the list aloud remind students of any other words?

**5.** Now you can assign the fire drill poem for students to write on their own. After each writing rush, have a few students read their lists aloud. Try doing this with key words from any lessons in math, science, or history. This is a good way to review vocabulary from past lessons.

**6.** Make a list poem by rearranging words or by adding the word *and* or *but* in between each pair of words. Then you can ask students to use these words in a form poem such as haiku, diamante, cinquaine, or sestina. Of course, the list can be used as material for just about any curriculum-related poem assignment from other sections of this book.

## SHOPPING LIST POEMS

Grades: 1–4

Cross-curricula: Math, Science

A group vocabulary and memorization exercise that is quick and fun is the shopping list poem. This exercise combines two of the greatest childhood desires: food and spending money. It also contains the curriculum content area of directions. It is along the lines of a jump-rope poem, which begins with a rhyming couplet and then counts down a list of words or numbers while someone jumps rope. For example: "Anna Banana played the piano. All she knew was the Star Spangled Banner. Anna Banana split, two, three, four, five, six, seven, eight . . ." The class can snap their fingers to keep time on their literary trip to the store. This is a poem for exploring humor, syllables, and rhythm.

Before you begin, make up your own memorable directions rhyme: "I'm going to the store for my mom and dad./I hope I still remember the list I had./Two blocks make a right/sharp left at the light./Up the hill down the way/this should not take all day: eggs, milk, bread . . ."

**1.** Begin with the class by writing a group rhyme on the board that describes the directions to the store. Ask the first three students for a one-syllable grocery item. Write these on the board beneath the rhyme. Have everyone say the poem together.

**2.** Have the next student say the poem and add a one-syllable grocery item to the end of the list.

**3.** As each student adds another item and says the poem over again, write the new word on the board. As usual, make sure that your scribe is writing down the poem from the board. Have each student add a word and repeat the poem aloud. When the list is complete, see if the class can write the return directions and still have them rhyme. When the group composition is complete, have students read it together, keeping time by snapping their fingers.

**4.** Now try a shopping list poem where students memorize the grocery list, as with the "I Remember You Poems" in Chapter 8 ("Human Values"). Begin by writing the group directions rhyme. Have the first student begin the grocery list, but this time with two- or three-syllable items. Each subsequent student says the whole poem, adding a new item at the end. Do this until the list is too long for the students to remember. Poets can "shop 'til they drop" and then start over.

The more unusual the items added by students, the funnier the poem becomes. Write the items down on a pad as they are added by the memory poets. Encourage the students to use the memorization techniques of picturing the words and saying them in a meter, or "to a beat."

If there are vocabulary words the class needs to memorize or study, you may want to send the students to a science store, a math mall, a grammar grab, or a health or computer sale, and have them recite the words from a given lesson. Ask them to include vocabulary words from previous lessons. Once you get into the fun of repetition and the chanting and cheering of list poems, you may also use sections of the phone book or the dictionary as a source.

Another version of this game can be played by older students with foreign language words, using directions and the shopping list. Since it is an oral exercise, students don't have to worry about spelling until later. The foreign language shopping list can use clothing and colors or animals and colors with the appropriate grades. And the poem can end by yelling a money amount (in francs, pesos, etc.) that the student estimates it would cost.

| | |
|---|---|
| *A la izquierda por la esquina* | Left at the corner |
| *A la derrecha hasta la luz* | Right at the light |
| *Un perro azul* | One blue dog |
| *Un cero rojo* | One red pig |
| *Un pajaro blanco* | One white bird |
| *Cuatro gatos negros* | Four black cats |
| *Dos pescados amarrillos* | Two yellow fish |
| *Veinte armadillos* | Twenty armadillos |
| *Tres tigres naranjas* | Three orange tigers |
| *Cien nuevo huesos* | One hundred new bones |
| *Ciento mil pesos* | One hundred thousand dollars |

—Aaren Yeatts Perry

## ALPHABET ACROSTIC

Grades: 1–6

Cross-curricula: All

In this exercise, each letter of the alphabet begins a word or phrase. The acrostic form may be written vertically or horizontally. Line up the letters vertically for the first few acrostics so that the words or phrases can be written across the board horizontally. Instead of a word, use the alphabet for the first group acrostic. Try to write half of the alphabet vertically down the left side of the board. The second half can be assigned for individual writing.

**1.** First explain to the class that in this writing exercise they are all living in the same house. This will be their chance to write about it. Usually someone will say, "Ew, gross! I could never live with Danny!" Then the fun begins. You may want to title the poem beforehand, discuss content, and make a story out of it. Or you may conduct the exercise and see what improvisation brings.

**2.** While you are writing the alphabet vertically on the board, ask students in their new house to begin thinking about what activities and games they do together, who cooks, what foods are popular, rooming arrangements, housekeeping rules, the type of house, the yard, and so on. "A" can begin, for example, either "an awesome afternoon at . . ." or "an awful afternoon at . . ." Leave some space between letters and use two chalkboard panels if need be.

**3.** Begin asking for words that start with the letters *A, B, C,* and so on. Prompt the students with good questions that can set them up.

**4.** Reexplain that the acrostic poem is about a house in which all of the children in the classroom live together and that you would like to have the students' help in using the alphabet to describe it. With younger students, you can help them through the whole alphabet. Older students can be helped halfway through the alphabet or until they get the idea, and then encouraged to finish the alphabet poem themselves.

**5.** If the students are offering phrases or single words, you may suggest conjunctions or leading questions that can connect the phrases into sentences. If the students are coming up with whole sentences, suggest shorter sequiturs that can help move the poem through a theme or story and toward a conclusion. With first- and second-grade students, ask for single words that students will recognize. Then you can suggest a preposition: "Boxes in the basement." This is a good time to practice alliteration by including as many words in a row as possible that begin with each letter. Again, you can prompt student imagination with simple questions: "Boxes where in the house? Boxes doing what that begins with 'B'? Making what kind of noise? With whom?"

**6.** With younger students, have them read through the poem with you. Ask your older students who wants to read his or her finished version of the alphabet acrostic. Ask the class if they want to suggest any revisions, both for the group section on the board and for the individual students' endings to the poem.

Another session can do the same thing with the A-to-Z of a recent field trip, students' neighborhoods, favorite foods, animals, or classroom subject matter. Students in the higher grades can write an acrostic poem describing characters or scenes in a story they have read, or specific lesson they've completed.

## CATERPILLAR POEMS

Grades: 1–3

Cross-curricula: Science

Word worms can be created in the same manner as in the preceding exercise. Simply by drawing a head at the beginning of a sentence and circling each word, making the circles touch, you can draw a caterpillar sentence, which turns into the butterfly of a poem when completed.

**1.** With first- and second-grade students, write a short rhyming poem about a nature topic that you are studying, or select one from your unit material.

**2.** Scatter the words to the short sentence randomly at the top of a photocopied worksheet. Below that, draw the caterpillar's empty circular or oval body sections, to be filled in with the words. The worm can be drawn vertically, horizontally, or in a slinky shape. Each section might contain the first or last letter of the word that goes there.

**3.** Begin by writing the first word on the board, and have students write the word in their first caterpillar section. Now ask who can find the second word. Of course, as the words are found and written one at a time into the caterpillar, deciding which word is next will be easier for students.

**4.** When the caterpillar sections are filled with the words to the poem, read the poem together with the class.

**5.** Now have students turn over the paper and rewrite the poem in the shape of a butterfly. You can predraw the insect and provide the lines to write on as part of the photocopied worksheet. Or you may have some cardboard template cutouts of butterflies that students can trace, writing the poem within the shape of the butterfly.

## MINUTE METAPHOR POEMS

Grades: 3–6

Teacher Julia Blumenreich recommends this exercise to other teachers when she is explaining how to get a class to understand and start using metaphors.

**1.** Guide students in creating the following lists on the board. You can make it as much like a magic formula as possible—have the students give you words from their current math or science lesson, or words that start with the same letter as their first or last names.

**2.** In three vertical columns, list 10 nouns, 10 colors, and 10 more nouns. Leave space between the first and second columns and at the end. Encourage student contributions to interpret both colors and nouns as broadly as possible. Colors can be *bubblegum pink* or *slate blue*. Nouns, rather than being only objects, can have the sweeping qualities of concepts—*disdain* or *memory* or *freedom*. (See the Compound Color Poem in Chapter 2, "Art.")

**3.** Now go through the list line by line and write, *is a* between the first noun and the color. This should give you some very poetic metaphors, like "Memory is a slate blue swan." With older students, you can make the nouns plural and change *is a* to *are* to get lines like "Memories are desert gold dogs" or "Trust is a bubblegum pink bicycle wheeling off the pier of friendship into a lake of laughter."

**4.** The last part can be written line by line as a group or assigned to the class for their solo work. Simply add the word *that* at the end of every line. "Memory is a slate blue swan that comes floating back to me at night, spreads its wings, and says . . ." With this part, the poets can take liberties with length and content. Even if you assign the 10 group metaphor lines that are on the board, each student will give them new and distinct meaning.

**5.** While working with tenses, try assigning the same poem using the past tenses—*was, has been, had been,* and *were*—and adding the word *until* at the end instead of *that*.

## RANDOM NOUNS AND VERBS

Grades: 3–6

Another exercise suggested by Julia Blumenreich involves making a list of 10 nouns on one sheet of paper and 10 verbs on another. The act of making common noun–verb combinations into randomly joined pairs creates poetic juxtapositions that can inspire students to, as Blumenreich puts it, "be free with their thinking and be O.K. with the experimentation process."

**1.** With the class, create some sample lists of nouns and verbs on the board. Here is a sample list of nouns: *Ping-Pong ball, computer, volcano, Bill of Rights, sweat, elephant, jar, candy, poetry, hockey puck*. Here are some verbs: *talk, cheat, spell, write, climb, fly, act, drink, evaporate, blow*.

**2.** When students get the idea, have them make their own lists. Tell them to keep their verbs and give their list of nouns to another student.

**3.** When students have the two lists in front of them, ask one of them to give you an example of the kind of combination he got when he followed his first noun with their first verb: "Ping-Pong balls talk."

**4.** After students have the pairs of words they will use, ask them to extend the noun–verb combinations into full sentences. With ten combinations they can use the five senses (sight, smell, taste, hearing, touch), the five questions (who, what, where, when, and why), and other items from their Self-Questioning Guide Sheet. Or they can use this as a simile or metaphor exercise. For example, "Ping-Pong balls talk in footsteps clomping like horses running sideways down a hollow street."

## MIGHTY MORPHEMES

Grades: 3–6

Cross-curricula: All

With poetic license, almost any word can become a *free morpheme*, a word that, when combined with one or two others, can create a new word. Better known as *compound words*, these simple linguistic equations can be a helpful and enjoyable way to study the reduction or increase in stress on familiar words as they are combined with others to make new ones.

**1.** Prepare a list of your own favorite compound words for the class. Discuss the concept of compounds with the class before making the assignment, and write some of your favorites on the board. How were certain compounds invented? By whom?

**2.** Either on the board or with students writing the words on their own papers, brainstorm a general list of compound words.

Categories are helpful for students as a place to look for compounds. You can use food, sports, or neighborhood landmarks. Words from popular songs, games, news stories, or television shows can be put to good use in this exercise. Words like *basketball, jumprope, daylight,* and *ice cream* are right on the tips of our tongues. If students offer words like *snow day,* or *push button,* use them as an opportunity to explain the inflection on *snow* and *push* and the reduced stress on *day* and *button.* You can affirm this observation with similar additional words, such as *snowman* or *pushover.* See if your list includes any hyphenated words. Explain the difference between two separate words, a hyphenated word, and a compound word.

**3.** Now brainstorm another list of curriculum-related compound words from, say, a science unit on geology or geography, in two columns. Which of these can you match with words from the opposite column to "morph" it into a compound word?

**4.** Try having students invent a couple of found poem stanzas or quatrains using three or four compound words. If they choose a specific topic such as a trip they took or a recent study area, they will have a place in their minds to look for the words. See how many triple words students can find, like *upside down*, and how many compound words can be generated around one topic. Encourage the use of more articles, pronouns, and connective words than in the following impacted poem:

> Airplane to grandmother's farmhouse.
> Too late. A daylight whitewash of
> snowflakes backflipping in midair
> blackout sunlight on the runway.
>
> —Aaren Yeatts Perry

## WORD BAG POEMS

Grades: 2–6

I have been conducting what McKim and Steinbergh call "Wordbowl"[3] poems for years. Before recycling old magazines, I cut out words and update my collection. I find that brown paper shopping bags work better than bowls in my classrooms, where the frenzy of tiny hands reaching for words calls for something that can be replaced. The thousands of words have survived and have been used in innumerable poetic combinations. I try to include good single words and short phrases containing every part of speech.

**1.** Start by cutting words out of magazines, tabloids, newspapers, anything with dynamic titles that has letters at least one-quarter inch in height. When you have compiled enough words so that each of your students will have an average of 10 to 30 words, you have enough to begin the Word Bag workshop. In their aforementioned book, McKim and Steinbergh also have pages of juicy, poetic, typed words that can be photocopied and cut out.

**2.** Each time you conduct the exercise, decorate another shopping bag. To build excitement when you begin, ask students to guess what's in the bag. Have them clear their desk except for a sheet of paper and a pencil. Explain that you are going to go around and place a small pile of words on each person's desk. Make sure you don't put down so many words that students can't sort them out. Start with 10 or 15 each.

**3.** If you would like to create a group sample poem on the board, write one of the student's collections of words on the board. Have them read the words to you one at a time. Write them randomly. Once the word list is complete, you can begin showing students the selection process that you would use. A bold word or phrase may jump out at you as a good title. Another strong word or phrase may make a good opening to the poem. Build sentences and phrases with the rest of the words. The poem may emerge with a magical meaning or with a nonsensical but poetic sequence of words.

**4.** Have students turn over all of their pieces of paper so that they can read each word clearly. Have them choose a word they think will be a good beginning to a poem and place that word at the top of their desk. What word makes sense after that in a sentence? And what word would logically connect with that one? Encourage them to keep adding words together until a poem starts to come out. This is a good time to tell them not to sneeze or laugh at the poem so as not to blow the words away.

This exercise is similar to playing a musical instrument by ear. Tie notes/words together in various sequences until they sound good/make meaning.

**5.** Circulate during this exercise to help students with questions and make suggestions. As soon as someone has something completed and wants to write it down, collect the students' remaining words and allow them to write. They will no doubt come back for more words.

**6.** Students will construct sentences or phrases using words whose meaning they don't know, but whose context is correct. Explain the meanings and use this exercise as a vocabulary builder. Also be prepared to explain the exercise to the parents of the students who create nonsensical versions.

**7.** Some of the poems will call for a revision and rewrite. People will be amazed at the poetics and at the age of the author. Other word bag poems may not make as much sense but are great writing and sequencing exercises.

*First Poet (Word Bag)*

The universe for me
a whoosh and a zonk
yes yes yes.
Released a number of
women changing society
in the interest of the
verbal dimension
won't you be,
sunset
dear.

—Jessica Melendez (Grade 3)

*Word Bag*

After so many years don't get
me wrong. Poetry pushes the
planet. There are always people
who have extra brain cells.

—Caesar Ocasio, Jayson Bahamonde (Grade 4)

## LIMERICKS

Grades: 3–6

Cross-curricula: Science, Social Studies

There are five simple rules that young writers should know about the limerick.

1. It is a story.
2. It has a specific rhythmic meter or pattern (usually anapestic).
3. It rhymes in an A-A-B-B-A pattern.
4. It is funny.
5. It is (usually a mockery or satire) about a person with a made-up or real name.

The last line not only should rhyme with the first but should be a revealing and well-crafted punch line. If a student shows a great interest in this form of poetry, challenge him or her to write as many as possible in the related English-language *trochaic* and *dactylic* meters.

**1.** First, write the rules on the board or pass out a sheet with the rules on one side and some blank lines on the other. Read several limericks to the class so they can internalize the rhythm and the rhyme scheme. Discuss what they notice about the poems as a way to get them to understand the rules.

**2.** Do a group limerick on the board about a famous person who appears in a social studies lesson: a president who fell down steps, a vice-president who couldn't spell, or a famous discoverer who got lost, a scientist, a doctor, a character in a story. It may make even more sense to students if the subject of the group limerick is a school principal or someone local and living.

**3.** Then have each student choose a person to write about. Have them write their own limericks by creating an imaginary character with an imaginary name who can embody some funny incident that they witnessed.

Edward Lear, who is credited with popularizing the form, published a whole book of limericks in 1864 called *Book of Nonsense*. The following two limericks, according to Cheney,[4] were composed by Lear. The third, from Norton, is anonymous[5]:

There was an old man in a tree,
Whose whiskers were lovely to see.
  But the birds of the air
  Plucked them perfectly bare,
To make themselves nests in that tree.

There is a young lady whose nose,
Continually prospers and grows.
  When it grew out of sight,
  She exclaimed in a fright,
"Oh, Farewell to the end of my nose!"

There once was a spinster of Ealing,
Endowed with such delicate feeling,
  That she thought an armchair
  Should not have its legs bare—
So she kept her eyes trained on the ceiling.

**4.** Review and rewrite these poems with attention to the form.

Of course, you can invent limerick games for your classroom. One is a round robin or assembly line approach to writing them in which each student writes a first line, "There once was a man/woman/boy/girl/person named whoever . . . ," then passes it to the next student for the second line, "Who thought he was terribly clever . . . ," and so on. Students listen to identify "their line" when the finished poems are read. Integrate information from whatever unit you are working on in science, math, or another content area.

The limerick is often a wicked and bawdy form of humor. Its propensity toward vulgarity, cynicism, and cutting humor is its very source of accurate and poignant description. The fact that it is a controlled and focused literary form is all the more reason for children to explore it.

## PROVERBS FROM HECK

Grades: 3–6

Another formula poem can be created by mimicking William Blake's "Proverbs from Hell." Certain lines contain a metaphor pattern that is easy for children to reproduce using their own knowledge and experience.

**1.** First ask students to help you make some lists. List 10 normal qualities or feelings (happiness, sadness, fear, hunger, joy, promptness, surprise, curiosity, jealousy, sympathy), then 10 animals, then 10 highly virtuous qualities or feelings, (justice, glory, sympathy, virtue, faith, love, trust, luck, fortune, will). Write these in vertical columns on the board as students do the same on their papers.

**2.** Place the word *of* between the first and second columns, the word *is* between the second and third column, and the words *of Joey* or *of Amy* (the name of the author) at the end.

**3.** You should now have the makings of lines like, "The jealousy of the snake is the hope of Joey" or "The imagination of the ant is the glory of Amy."

**4.** After writing these in columns on the board and constructing a few group versions taking suggestions from the class, ask students to write 5 to 10 of their own.

## PARALLEL POEMS

Grades: 3–6

Cross-curricula: Science

Also common to all people of the world are parallels. These are lines of poetic wisdom, universal truths passed down through the ages, in which the second line either agrees with or contrasts with the first. They are a great form of compare-and-contrast poem. Part of their lasting legacy lies in the truth they speak, part in their pithy phraseology. They are excellent practice for the ability to write "free verse" and expository prose.

*Synonymous parallels* impart the same wisdom in two different ways. The first line states a truism, and the second repeats the thought in different words. "Let your poems speak unabashed truths and let your rhymes ring clear as thunder." "Love your neighbor with the wreath of work and play as you would love your brother in another country with commerce and culture." "The good student gets straight 'A's' and he writes good poems."

In *antithetic parallels* the first line delivers the same profound truism. The second line states a view that is exactly opposite of the first line, in an effort to prove the same point: "The good poem will be spoken by many, where the bad poem is heard by few." "A bad student will stay in the afternoon to clean the boards, but a good student is he who dirties them with poems in the morning."

Religious literature is full of synonymous parallels, from the Proverbs of Solomon, to the laws in the Talmud, to the Koran and the Buddhist and Hindu texts. Better examples for children can be found in nursery rhymes, street sayings, and the ones we invent.

Have students make their own parallel poems relating to schoolwork, parents, rules at home, traffic rules, or things they know about sports, favorite or worst foods, or animals.

**1.** Discuss the rules of parallels and create some group samples on the board with the class in, for example, a science content area. "It is the land that feeds the river mud, but it is bad farming that darkens the waters with lost soil."

**2.** Review your recent science lesson and write some of the facts on the board, such as a few examples of water, land, air, and noise pollution. As you are asking the class to recall to you the information from the lesson, ask them also to begin to imagine statements of opposing or agreeing wisdom about these science facts. "It is the raging river that we drink from but it is the river that thirsts for a clean drink."

**3.** Assign your students two to four synonymous or antithetic parallels. Have them write on their own in the content area you have outlined. When they are finished, have a reading to see how many included both science data and a good parallel statement: "Each city sends a message with the fish in the river as it goes to sea, but the ocean cannot hear dead fish talking."

**4.** Tell students to star or asterisk the one that works the best. Tell them to extend the parallel and keep writing either matching or opposing poetic statements. "The ocean listens for a new message way down stream but we have only told the angry ocean to be quiet."

## TALL TALE POEMS

Grades: 1–4

Start by explaining the tradition of the tall tale. You might explain that a tall tale is in the same family as the legend, the myth, and the fantasy story. The tall tale has been made famous by such noted stories as "John Henry," "Paul Bunyan," and more recently "Swamp Annie."

Begin with some sentences fictionalizing your own day at school so that your students get a good sense that it's O.K. to create fiction in this way. Then have students create a fictional day at school. Add phrases or lines that evoke the drama, urgency, guilt, confidence, authority, and verity of the tall tale.

Several of the lie poems in Kenneth Koch's *Wishes, Lies, and Dreams* are poems that tell lies about where the child has been. There are references to and interpretations of all the curricular areas.

**1.** For individual tall tales, ask students to start with some places that they go regularly or that they have visited recently. Go around the room and ask for hands of those who are ready to tell a tall tale about something that happened recently in one of those places.

Tall tales can inspire creative writing in several ways, not the least of which is competition among classmates. "Sitting around in a group," says Koch, ". . . they try to top each other with statements stranger and more fantastic than the ones they've heard so far. . . . I ask the children to put a lie in every line," explains Koch, "or else just to make up a whole poem in which nothing was true."[6]

**2.** Now that you are warmed up, create a group composition on the board in which you begin to get far more extravagant. Decide whether you are writing a poem that is a tale meant to be believed or one that is a fantastic lie. Either or both can be poetic. Ask for statements that make sense as sentences and phrases.

**3.** Tell your students to go ahead and write their own tall tales to have fun with them, to make them wild and excessive and bold. Again, tell them to decide whether it is a fantastic painting of an impossible tale or a tale meant to be believed. Just asking this of the students will result in incredibly imaginative paragraphs of writing. Either way, students should be told to focus less on the *and then . . . and then . . . and then. . .* of the story and more on the words that describe the places and actions and things in the story.

**4.** Do a reading of the lies with dramatization. I have also asked students who were stuck (and said they "couldn't lie"!) to write tall tale poems in certain contexts. For example, have students assume they have been away from home for a long time. Their parents are worried about where they have been. The lie they write has to convince the parent or parents, for example, that they really did see an eagle get shot out of the sky and went to save it, or that they really did get lost on a new motorcycle and ended up in California and can describe the landscape there!

The poem can be written in the story format or in some poetic permutation of a tale, like repeating "Believe me! Believe me!" or "Imagine this . . ."

Another context from which to work is the "Tale That Changed My Life," or ". . . That Changed the World." All of these may take on the guilty connotations of a lie or the exclamatory dimensions of a tall tale. Try to have them bring out the specific emotion of the poem.

## THE THINGS LETTERS TELL ME

Grades: 1–3

What does the sound of a letter do to help a student remember its use? One way of helping students remember how to write letters and words is by introducing them to the *onomatopoeia*: forming a word by imitating the sound of its action or object.

**1.** Ask the class to give you words that start with the letter they describe. With younger students you can use the simile "G sounds *like* . . ." or "W is *like* whistling in the wind."

**2.** Say the letter to the class. Then have the class say it as pronounced and as loudly as possible.

**3.** Rather than simply asking students for a word that begins with the letter, try to get them to imagine what the letter sounds like. The vowels preceding or following many consonants are a good place to go looking for imaginative meanings in letters: *W* being spelled with whole words, and *G* being followed by two *e*'s.

**4.** After writing each letter on the board and having the class play vocally with the letter's sound, write the poetry comparison phrase on the board. "*W* sounds like crossing your eyes and seeing blue bubbles. *G* can gurgle in the throat like a frog gagging or jump like an aging gargoyle from the garage." Indulging in selected letters is better than trying to get through the whole alphabet at one time.

**5.** Use the finished poem as a read-along lesson to explore the range of letter pronunciations with the whole class.

With older students you can use the same approach as with the alphabet acrostic and encourage the use of alliteration as well. Try to chain together as long of a sentence as possible for each letter: "*C* can crowd countless chapters crying cacophonous cat calls."

## POETRY DICTIONARY ACTIVITY

Grades: 2–6

If students invent any new onomatopoeic words in their writing exercises, these words can be entered into a poetry dictionary. Making entries into their own dictionaries helps students learn how to alphabetize, identify syllables, and read the standard dictionary.

If your classroom has computers, a poetry dictionary is a valuable and fun activity for keyboard-happy students. If you find yourself referring to these electronic dictionaries often enough, you may want to keep an updated file called Poetry Encyclopedia, containing an ever-expanding list of feelings and emotions, poetry technique tools, rules for forming poems, the Self-Questioning Guide Sheets, and bibliographies of poetry books for children.

For newly invented words, set up a form for students on which the invented word is spelled in capital letters with the syllables divided, as with a regular dictionary, followed by the letter for noun, verb, adjective, and so on, depending on your grade level. Number the definitions if an invented word inspires more than one. This is a good exercise to turn to when a student says he "can't explain it." Have him invent a word that approximates his feeling.

The following is a related writing exercise for the invention of new letters, consonants, and vowels for your poetry dictionary.

**1.** First go down the alphabet and explain that consonants are air trapped or stopped by the mouth when it makes different shapes, and that vowels are air that is released but guided and shaped by the mouth.

**2.** Ask students to hold their breath briefly and to release it by making a new letter. How do the new letters sound? How are they spelled? Can the new letter be added to standard letters to create a new word? This is a good time to explain diphthongs to grades 5 and 6.

**3.** As the students write the new letters and words on the board, you can help by writing out the invented definitions next to them.

**4.** When you have a list of new words, request that students write a stanza or short paragraph story telling the tale of the words' and letters' discovery.

Interested students can enter all of the tool box inventory into this poetry dictionary as they learn about the tools. If students know that they can look up tools, forms, and other definitions here, they may be more likely to begin writing on their own when poem or story ideas occur to them.

## ASSEMBLY LINE POEMS

Grades: 3–6

**1.** Give each student a paper containing a key word or phrase that ends with a different letter. The key word can come from a recent lesson in any curricular area. Have the first poet write a connecting word or phrase beginning with the ending letter of your initial word. Also have the first poet write his or her name on the back of the paper, as it will return to the student at the end of the exercise.

**2.** When the first round of students are finished, have them pass papers in an orderly direction. Continue having each consecutive student write a word that begins with the last letter of the previously written word, and then pass it on. Students can be encouraged to add a word or phrase that makes sense thematically and builds a sentence-based text, or to improvise freely and build a nonlinear collage.

**3.** When all students have written a connecting word, the piece should be returned to the student whose name is written on the back. Have the students read the poem. Give them time to make minor revisions and interpret others' handwriting.

**4.** Start asking if any students are willing to read their poems aloud. Some will find their poems too nonsensical; others will have more highly evolved poems. But once students have heard one another's versions, they should be more willing to read their own.

## JOURNAL WRITING

Grades: 1–6

Writing creatively and freely every day primes the pump. It keeps open the mind's physiological channel to the hand and the paper. When journal-writing students are asked to write a poem, they are ready. They associate the act of writing with relief, not pain. They are familiar with their own voice, techniques, and tools. They are not inhibited because they have not been censored or criticized but encouraged. They have experienced self-affirmation from journal writing and peer verification from poetry readings. Because they have already done a lot, they feel they can do a little more. They have, if only out of habit, developed a need for language and writing.

Journal writing is a form of self-monitoring that prepares students for basic self-expression. "Journal writing, along with other forms of writing," conclude Palmer, Hafner, and Sharp, "helps students develop their abilities as thinkers; that is, they practice analyzing, synthesizing and evaluating as they construct meaning while writing."[7]

While journaling capitalizes on the benefits of good habits, it moves the need to write from habitual to conscious, from repetitive to responsive, from mundane to meaningful. The constant beginning, middle, and end of the sentence, the affirming indulgence in simple thoughts, the uncensored struggle to articulate complex feelings, call forth the body's natural desire to communicate well.

Journaling is a wake-up exercise equivalent to stretching for dancers, sketching for visual artists, and arpeggios for musicians. If a student can play arpeggios on the piano every day, that discipline can bring forth creativity. Journal writing is the arpeggio of creative writing. Many great poems are begun here.

This is another important place for parents and teachers to get involved with the creative writing process. If this kind of writing is combined with good instruction and parental support, students will have a great chance of bringing their own creative work to life in the world. Having a conversation with a child in grades 1 through 3 and making a brief journal entry of the things the child says can become part of the child's record of creative development as well as a memento of the parent–child relationship.

I have kept journals since I was in the fifth grade. I have over 30 hardback Strathmore sketchbooks, at 220 pages each, that I have filled with poems, dreams, and essays wedged in among the what-I-did-today pages. "The craft demands," says poet Lamont Steptoe, "that we write and write and write some more."[8]

## SESTINAS

Grades: 3–6

The sestina is a poem of 39 lines with a repeating line formula. The sequences are too long for students to memorize, so you can begin this type of poem and then work on it in more than one session if necessary. It is included here because it requires students to think about a series of words in sustained writing, and to develop precision in language by creating many different approaches to the same words. The sestina is fun to make and gives students a sense of accomplishment in a group poem format.

The idea of the poem is to use the same six words repeatedly in a different order, always at the end of a line. You may choose to use six different colors, six teachers' or students' names, six days of the week, or six examples of a science, math, or social studies concept.

It helps most students to have the numbers written at the end of each line on the board or on photocopied worksheets.

The sequence is 123456, 615243, 364125, 532614, 451362, 246531. The last stanza has three lines, each of which have two end words: 2 and 5, 4 and 3, 6 and 1.

## NOTES

1. Hillary-Anne Farley, "This Is a Poem," in Richard Lewis, ed., *Miracles: Poems by Children of the English-speaking World* (New York: Simon & Schuster, 1966), p. 14.

2. Elizabeth McKim and Judith Steinbergh, *Beyond Words: Writing Poetry with Children* (Greenharbor, MA: Wampeter Press, 1983), p. 45.

3. Ibid., p. 37.

4. Arnold Cheney, *The Poetry Corner* (Glenview, IL: Good Year Books, 1984), p. 41.

5. Anonymous, *The Norton Introduction to Poetry* (New York: W. W. Norton, 1986), p. 159.

6. Kenneth Koch, *Wishes, Lies, and Dreams* (New York: Harper & Row, 1970), p. 198.

7. Barbara C. Palmer, Mary L. Hafner, and Marilyn F. Sharp, eds., *Developing Cultural Literacy through the Writing Process: Empowering All Learners* (Boston: Allyn and Bacon, 1994), p. 240.

8. Lamont B. Steptoe, *Mad Minute* (Philadelphia: Whirlwind Press, 1994).

# 4

# Health

This book can only begin to address some of the complex issues relating to bodily awareness and health within the elementary curriculum. At every stage of development, from childhood through adolescence, one's body is a source of many questions. If these questions are ignored, students will fill in the blanks with misleading answers. These poetry-writing exercises offer strategies to increase bodily awareness and self-expression by encouraging a healthy, scientific, and "biological" approach.

## CLEAN AS A WHISTLE

Grades: 1–3

With a first-grade class discussing health issues of body cleanliness, a group poem can be written on the board and then spoken aloud with the class. It helps if you devise a chorus about body hygiene and repeat it while clapping with the class between the stanzas the group creates: "I scrubbed myself from head to toe with a brush that only had one bristle. Now I'm happy from head to toe, because I'm cleeee-an as a whistle." Then go over the body, making similes about the clean and the dirt for each area: "My toes were as dirty as ticket stubs, now they're clean as scoured-out tubs." There is no guarantee that this will change those children that hate taking baths, but it's worth a try.

## DEAR ME POEMS

Grades: 3–6

This exercise is similar to Canfield and Wells's "Letter from the Interior,"[1] in which they suggest having students "pretend their body could write them a letter." They suggest brainstorming and discussing what different areas of the body would say to the individual about how they're being treated.

Write another poem in which different parts of the body either whisper or scream to the writer something that they either like or dislike about the way they're being treated. Some parts will calmly whisper "thank-you's" or "don't worry's" or secrets to other parts. Some parts will yell angry rhymes, metaphors, and similes at others. This type of exercise gets the best results if it is a surprise assignment. The poem is based on the vibrant moments when one is pretending. What words can the students hear the body saying—dreams, sounds, stories, invitations?

Some visually inclined students enjoy giving a tour of their bloodstream, their mind, or the landscape of their body, à la "Journey to the Center of the Earth."

*Visit My Lips*

My lips are so dry
that they are like
a desert.
If you shrunk and
walked on my lips
man, you die walking
weeks and weeks with
no water.
That's how dry each
of my lips are.
That's what happens
to people who visit
my lips.

—David (Grade 4)

## I LIKE MY TOES

Grades: 3–6

I have done this exercise many times with different grades. But I had never heard such a good model poem as this one by singer/songwriter John Gorka. It is excerpted here:

*Body Parts Medley*

I like my feet. They're very neat.
No one can compete with the meat in my feet.
I like my toes. We're very close.

I should compose epic prose for my toes.
They hold up my legs while shopping for eggs.
Now everyone begs to have pegs like my legs.
I keep my calves around for laughs.
Both of my halves take their baths with my calves.
I like my thighs. They're just the right size.
They help me rise to new highs, my two thighs. . . .

—John Gorka*

Ask students to match Gorka's challenging rhyme scheme (a rhyming couplet in the first line and three rhymes in the second) with as many lines about other body parts as possible. To provide a vocabulary source and a subject focus, you may want to connect this writing exercise with a lesson from a nutrition, disease, or environmental health unit: "Well, I like fresh air, my lungs breath it like a bear. You might not care, but smoking gives me a scare, my lungs like fresh air."

## BODY ODE

Grades: 2–6

A paean, ode, or praise poem to one body part will inspire very descriptive writing.

**1.** Ask students to make a list of the 10 things they like the most about their body. This list can include things that the body can do as well as ways the body looks and feels.

**2.** Have a student read her list aloud. As you write these items on the board, think about which one would be appropriate for a haiku. Choose one from the list that the student seems to like the most and ask her to expound on it. What about it does she like? What does her nose do that is like something else? What is it shaped like? What does it feel like?

My eyes are so cute.
My eyes are so incredible
My eyeballs are big

—Lydia Suarez (Grade 4)

**3.** The preceding haiku could be expanded into a tanka poem simply by adding two more seven-syllable lines. What about her eyes is cute? Is there something special that stands out? They are so cute because . . . ? When are they the cutest? Your eyeballs are as big as what? Ask students to build the descriptions of the thing they like the most into a poem with more details.

**4.** Now have the students write some lines addressing the body part they like the most. A beginning can address the part like a letter, "Dear Arm," or as if yelling: "Hey Hand!" Also suggest that they can begin every line with the traditional "Oh" or "Ah," which evokes the feeling of praise and allows the reader to understand the writer's emotional connection to the object. These praise lines can say not only what they like about the part but how much they need it. "Oh, hand, you chunky appendage of flesh and bones, sometimes clumsy, sometimes smooth as water. Please don't get caught in the door anymore. I need your strength, your spidery arpeggios to play the piano. I need you both to applaud."

## SAFETY ZONE POEMS

Grades: 3–6

This writing exercise is about language and safety. By the second grade, most students will know safety rules and procedures for bicycles, traffic, swimming, weather, injuries, fire, crime, poison, appliances, tools, medicine, siblings, animals, toys, electricity, water, strangers, school, playground, and hazardous substances.

A safety zone can be a mental place where one is safe. Students can create a rhyme or song to help remember how to get to their safety zone. The poem can be a jumprope chant about the safety precautions one takes when confronted with danger.

**1.** Review all the safety rules the students know so far, from both home and school. Write them on the board.

**2.** Write a sample poem in which the body cries to do the exciting but unsafe thing, but the mind catches it and says, "Safety Zone." Make up a few catch phrases like "safety zone" ("safety first," "heads up," "think twice," "stop-look-listen," etc.), and choose one for the sample group poem composed by the class.

*Running*

When I'm at the pool my body says, run!
Then my mind says, hey body, safety zone.
You can walk to the water and still have fun.

The fire alarm rings and my body does the splits!
Then my mind says, walk body, safety zone.
Hold hands on the way out and keep your wits.

—Aaren Yeatts Perry

**3.** Ask each student to choose a catch phrase and a safety issue and to write a rough draft of his own.

**4.** Have students read their drafts aloud. Encourage students to do a voice exercise where they yell the "body" part of the script (dramatize the excitement) and then whisper the "mind's" rational voice of safety.

**5.** When revising, make sure the poems still focus on safety. Some may drift from the issue in trying to complete a rhyme or stanza.

You can always devise your own rhyme scheme or form to fit your class. Limericks can also be tiny parables about safety. "There once was a boy who liked matches," and so on. A dialogue poem can focus on the words the body says to the child when trying to get him to break the rules and go outside the Safety Zone.

Of course, each "zone" has more than one rule to write about (e.g., swimming: don't eat first, buddy system, running, diving, etc.).

## INJURY POEMS

Grades: 2–6

All children love comparing personal injury stories. In this exercise we ask students to describe the moments and the story of the injury without telling what the injury was. Try to create a context in which each story is taken seriously but not overglorified.

**1.** Ask each student to list three injuries they can remember having or witnessing. Next to each of them, have them write the names of three surprise feelings they experienced when the incident occurred. You might brainstorm some accident-related surprise feelings on the board, such as shocked, frightened, nauseated, numb, nervous, tired, and shaken. How long did the accident take? How long did it appear to take?

**2.** Now ask them to tell the whole story. Make sure they include a description of the moment when they felt those surprise feelings. It's O.K. if students have to write out a longer version first and then edit out lines. The point is to get to the action moments just before, during, and after the unexpected accident: "Pumping down the street on my bike. Neck and neck with my brother. The store only a block ahead. Total freedom. I yelled, "I'm gonna beat ya. I'm fast as a cheetah.' Then the sudden game hunter's trap of the car door flung open. One last moment of flight before the baseball bat of the street against my head and shoulder. The fire of cement ripping into my skin. My screams curdled the milk I was supposed to take home to Mom. My bike looked like my bones felt—bent metal and spokes sticking out. But my bones, strong as desert wood, mending themselves inside, were getting ready to ride again."

**3.** After reading the stories back, students can be encouraged to sculpt them down into tighter, more poetic stanzas. Single words and incomplete phrases can evoke the urgency of accident. What were the most important moments? What words would you take out if you rewrote this story with just the action phrases, the scene description, the key words from the dialogue, and the surprise feelings? This shorter, more intense version will still tell the story but will condense it into a form more like the actual incident.

*"Illness or injury gives you a greater vulnerability—but it can also give a deeper sense of compassion for yourself and others."*—Linda Noble Topf[2]

## ABILITIES POEMS

Grades: 1–6

Preactivity Class Reading: "He Sees through Stone," by Etheridge Knight[3]

The following poem was written by a student in Michelle Kauffman's fifth grade at Huey Elementary School. Poet in residence Thelma Sheldon Robinson had brought a physically challenged poet to visit the classroom. What he shared with the class was informative and inspirational.

*Kevin Brown*

Kevin Brown is his name.
He knows how to rhyme words plain.
He is a poet by gift.
When he writes a poem, I get a lift.
For he is a blind man, he can't see.
When I hear his poems,
he brings out the positive in me.
To have a gift even though you are blind
can put a lot of thought in my young mind.

—Isiah Ulmer (Grade 5)

After having the following interaction with your class you might assign a poem similar to the above—a poem expressing wonderment, curiosity, understanding; an ode; a "they said he couldn't but he did" legend; or an "if I were blind" poem.

**1.** After discussing the lives of physically challenged people and their feelings and concerns, tell students that you would like to invite someone who is physically challenged into the classroom. Discuss the difference between having this visitor as a spectacle and having him as a normal guest. Brainstorm a list of questions. Ask students how they would feel if they were in a wheelchair, used crutches, or had a terminal or chronic illness. Try to develop the list of questions from what students do not know about illness and injury.

**2.** Bring a person who is wheelchair-bound or otherwise physically handicapped into the classroom. Try to locate someone who lives in the school community and who is also an artist or poet. Have the guest begin by telling the class about her profession, hobbies, interests, and family life, as you would with any other visitor. Perhaps the visitor is willing to explain more about her disability. It is helpful for the class if she is able to explain the phenomenon of discrimination: people laughing at differences; the idea that everyone has a disability; and, for older students, the difference between *sympathy* and *empathy*, what they mean and how best to help.

Encourage a discussion or question-and-answer period in which students can ask prewritten or impromptu questions. Most students will automatically have something to write in their journals about this.

**3.** This interaction and writing process helps to demystify, reduce fear, and normalize interaction between physically challenged and nonhandicapped students. It can also be a part of a longer term study of disabilities and healing. Make sure that learning outcomes include the ability to identify alternative methods of mobility and bodily functions for physically challenged people, and the manner or method in which the person found strength to do what she wanted to do in life. One East Coast quadriplegic plays the keyboard with her tongue.

For follow up, bring the same person back to the classroom at a later date to hear the students' poetry and comment on it. If this is not possible, poems can be sent in the mail. Correspondence, as with the Pen Pal Poems in the Social Studies chapter (Chapter 7), is something that excites most students.

**4.** Finally, with new awareness of ability and disability, students can write poems of great appreciation about the simplest of their peers' abilities.

**5.** On the board, brainstorm a list of positive adjectives and adverbs: *gracefully, smoothly, beautiful, like the wind, magically, strong, swiftly, balanced, kindly, like a giant, like a song*. Make a separate list on the board of qualities that include normal, day-to-day functions along with extraordinary abilities.

**6.** Choosing a peer from the classroom, each student can make a list of the things he or she likes most or will most remember about that peer. Then, removing the words "I like," students will be left with poetic phrases like "the way he blinks like a baby smiling."

**7.** Have the poets combine their lists to make a poem about their anonymous subject. The person's actions and their descriptions can be joined with *like* or *with*. These can be either very serious ("The way she walks smoothly like clouds moving past the sun," "The way she stands on one leg like the sun behind the clouds") or humorous ("The way his ears stay on his head with might and majesty, like sea shells staying in the ocean of his wavy hair listening to the music of the spheres").

## CARE PACKAGE POEMS

Grades 1–6

Preactivity Class Reading: "Right to Die" by William Stafford[4]

The same type of interaction and writing exercises can be done with victims of any terminal illness as in the disabilities poem. Connecting a human face with the topic always helps academic understanding and the ability to recapitulate learning in writing. This is a crucial step in diffusing or eliminating fear-based discrimination.

Many curriculum resources are being developed to talk about various diseases and illnesses. This writing activity can be integrated into any lesson on diseases or other health concerns.

The pen pal poems would work well here if you can make arrangements with a hospice, hospital, or local AIDS support organization. There are many excellent death and dying poems in the anthology *Life on the Line: Selections on Words and Healing*,[5] some of which are quite appropriate for elementary students.

**1.** Try an exercise in which students put things into the poem that can keep patients alive, as if the poem were a package. Make a list of containers or things that can contain or carry other things: box, shoe, vase, cup, bucket, squirrel's cheek, kangaroo's pouch, sky, trunk, pocket, valley, orbit, ship.

**2.** Begin the poem by stating what kind of container it is ("a duffle bag"). Begin every line with "This poem . . .": "This poem has everything you need to play every sport." "This poem has your size sneakers in it." "This poem has orange mango shower gel." "This poem is holding socks that just came out of the dryer, smelling like sprinklers in spring."

**3.** If students finish early they can take turns writing about different containers, filling each one with items in a metaphorical care package.

## TIRED POEMS

Grades: 2–6

Preactivity Reading: Pablo Neruda's "Walking Around"[6]

**1.** When discussing sleep, fatigue, and what makes the body tired, ask students what makes them tired. Ask about the distinction between being physically tired and being tired of something (bored).

**2.** Offer the class the chance to write a poem about what they are tired of. Make a list on the board of some of the things the students in your class are tired of doing. Then make another list of the things done by certain material objects when they are tired: books, doors, buildings, roofs, faucets, beds, wind, clouds, water, fire, dirt, light, dark.

**3.** How can they best describe the things that repeatedly tire them out? See if they can express dramatically the frustration of being tired of something when they read the poem.

**4.** Try having them add a line at the end about what they would rather be doing.

*Tired*

I'm tired of being at school.
I'm tired of multiplying.
I'm tired of adding.
I'm tired of subtracting.
I'm tired of dividing.
I'm so tired I'm going to
go home and bug my mom.

—Davine Enriquez (Grade 4)

## MAGIC POTION POEMS

Grades: 3–6

Cross-curricula: Science

Preactivity Class Reading: Zora Neal Hurston's *Sanctified Church*[7]

The "cures" listed in Zora Neal Hurston's book on African-American culture may or may not be practiced in your community. The following workshop is not meant to question or condone these beliefs and practices but to allow students to experiment with an informative, recipe mode of poetry writing, and to play a healthy game of "doctor" with words.

The cure for "night sweats," according to Hurston's research in the southern United States, suggests that "a bowl of water placed beneath the head of the sufferer for nine straight nights is thought to effect a cure." For tuberculosis: "Alligator tail, especially prepared, and water that has accumulated in old pine tree stumps . . . . Also the meat of fattened dogs killed by stealth."[8] While some cures may be seen as superstitions, others will be familiar to the class as serious remedies. Almost all the fourth graders in four different North Philadelphia third-grade classes knew it was important to put a penny on the forehead of someone with a nosebleed, but none of them had ever heard about "dropping a set of keys down the back" of someone with a bad case of hiccoughs.

**1.** During a Health unit on personal health, nutrition, diseases, and hygiene, students can be asked to talk about cures they have experienced either working or not working. To spark a prewriting discussion, compare experiences at the doctor's office and at the hospital. How were students treated? How did they get well again? Have the students take turns reading Hurston's cures one at a time. If a copy of this out-of-print book is not available, try inventing your potions based on the folk wisdom you have available in your classroom.

**2.** List on the board the illnesses and cures the students know about and have witnessed. Make a separate list of the diseases and illnesses for which there are still no cures. Talk about how doctors are constantly experimenting with new solutions. Is there anyone in the room who will become famous for discovering a vaccine or curing cancer? Ask if anyone knows how these diseases were treated in the past. Do cures or potions exist for social ills? Are they successful?

**3.** Put as many colors, animals, places, practices, and instructions in the poem as possible. But also help the students make them at least somewhat believable. Part of the fun of this exercise is coming up with the verbal part of the imagined panacea. This is what makes a good instructive or "informative" poem.

**4.** When the poets revise and edit their potion poems, have them repeat the verbal parts for oral presentation. Make sure they can read the poem aloud with a straight face, as if they are talking to a patient.

The aforementioned book, edited by another great poet, Toni Cade Bambara, also contains wonderful folktales like "Uncle Monday" and "Daddy Mention," as well as African beliefs related to birth and death, some of which are good inspiration for writing ghost stories.

> *"Disease can propel us forward because it gives us a much deeper understanding of the human spirit."*
>
> —Linda Noble Topf[9]

## GET WELL POEMS

Grades: 2–4

When a child in the class is out sick for a long period of time, bonds, friendships, and the sense of security among other students can be broken. Like the care package poems, a get well poem can be sent to the ailing student either in group form by the whole class or individually, as with get well cards.

**1.** After discussing the student who is out sick, have each student write down 5 to 10 things they like about the student. Use one student's list as an example and, staying true to the honest feelings of the writer, turn the complimentary lines into similes and metaphors where possible.

**2.** Then have the class write the repeating lines into a poem. Each line might begin with, "We miss the way you . . ." or "Get well soon/fast so that you can . . . again."

**3.** Another approach to this type of poem is the prayer or well-wishing phraseology: "May you be healed soon so that . . . "; "May you return to the spring sunlight so that we can have you on our kickball team again . . ."

**4.** Your students may want to write a more personal letter. Another option for a poem at the fifth- and sixth-grade levels is a study review poem. In the Health curriculum, for example, each student can remind the missing student of the material covered in a "Don't Forget" or "Remember" poem.

**5.** Each line of repeated rhyming couplets about a study area begins with "Remember . . ." For example, "Remember what we learned about substance abuse. Remember, if need be, you can always refuse. Remember when in pain and feeling unstable, don't take anything without reading the label."

## BODY COLORS

Grades: 1–5

Cross-curricula: Art

Bodies have many colors and tones that are not obvious at a glance. On closer inspection of hands, faces, teeth colors, hair, eyes, nails, and so on, students will find many subtle colors to write about. This writing exercise can help awaken descriptive powers and bodily awareness. It can also give students more background when discussing discrimination on the basis of appearance.

**1.** First ask students for a list of things on themselves that have color. Try to encourage the use of colors other than black and white.

**2.** When you have a list of body parts and colors on the board, ask students to help you extend the descriptions into similes and metaphors, and to compare the colors to objects in the world. For example: "My knuckles are as red as cherry tomatoes." "My two scars are as pink as tattoos."

**3.** Once they understand from the examples the depths of color and visual variety they consist of, ask them to revise and edit a finished poem to include as many colors as possible.

**4.** Another approach, for the rewriting stage, is to ask the poets to substitute "I am . . ." for "My hands are . . . " In this approach to bodily awareness, the body is seen as a whole rather than isolated parts.

*Green, Yellow, Blue*

As I look at myself, I like the color I see.
My favorite color is yellow, you see.
I'm happy and warm and it's the color of corn.

My other favorite color,
the best I've seen,
is a dark, hairy green.
It's the color of grass
And the color of trees.
It's the color of spinach
and the color of peas.
I'm happy, I'm soft,
I'm glad I'm not you.
Cause my other favorite color
is a bright yummy blue.
Like my good friend Aris
and my friend David, too,
when I look at that color,
I'm glad that its' blue!

—Alonzo Simmons, Jr. (Grade 3)

Allow students to go to the mirror to see if there are other colors they hadn't noticed before or to be more specific with the color names. A Caucasian child may find his skin tone to be a pink or peach color. An African-American child might find browns, yellows, chocolates, even blues. These exercises can help children develop an ability to see themselves clearly, less objectively, and to distinguish between literal and figurative appearance.

If a child comes up with a negative image or comparison, discuss it. Ask if this is what he means and feels. Are there other words that could say more accurately what he or she means? Is this how he wants the poem to portray him? He is in control. Try to encourage positive self-image thinking, but be careful not to censor harmless exploration.

## CHAKRA POEMS

Grades: 2–6

Cross-curricula: Social Studies, Science

In the ancient Ayurvedic medicine science of India, there are seven energy centers along the middle line of the human body. These are called *chakras*. Each *chakra* has a different color and physical quality. The top of the head, the forehead or "third eye," the throat, the heart, the belly, the pelvis, and the perineum are all focused on in the health practices of breathing and visual circulation of light.

Kenneth Koch refers to this second chakra or third-eye poem as "a magic power poem." Koch suggests having the kids "imagine they had a third eye in the middle of their foreheads and to say what it would see. The rule was that the third eye could see what the two regular eyes could not see and was only open when they were closed."[10]

Poetry-writing possibilities are endless: being able to see other cities or states, the countries of one's ancestors, scenes from myths, oneself in the future or in a "past life," objects in another place, molecular dinosaurs, the other side or inside of a wall, the inside of a rock, heart, cloud, or fruit—anything that cannot be seen with the naked eye. The content theme that you set for the writing assignment will determine the types and qualities of images.

**1.** Another such color imagination exercise is to close your eyes in front of the class and come up with a few of your own examples, writing them on the board as you go. Then have a student do the same thing in front of the class, freely relating to you the images that come across the screen of the mind's eye.

**2.** Colors can also be explored as a way of describing one's inner strength and personality. Ask the class for colors they think are connected to certain emotions. Look through your feelings and emotions list in your Poetry Dictionary, Tool Box, or Poetree House and write these on the board as you go through the questioning. What color is surprise? What color is relief, frustration, happiness?

**3.** After they get the idea, have students list 10 feelings and write a line or stanza for each feeling explaining what color they feel inside themselves when they feel this way.

**4.** Now give the class a more specific suggestion of content area. For each color–feeling combination, have students add an object that is that color.

"When I feel blue I am a silver icicle waiting to thaw." "When I am proud I am shiny purple and green with yellow stripes like the houses in my neighborhood." "When I am embarrassed I'm as red as an orange sunset." "When I am mad I am a red wagon burning rubber squealing around the corner to the pool to put out the fire."

## BODY ACROSTIC

Grades: 1–4

Cross-curricula: Science

Students can write a list of similes comparing any one of the bodily functions to different types of weather or geophysical activities. Now put the similes in an Acrostic poem about the bodily function. Let the title emerge from within each student's poem. Encourage the use of as many tools as possible.

> Heat in my heart mashes like molten magma
> Every pump pushing blood from my core
> Almost like a volcano erupting once more
> Right towards the mountain top of my brains.
> Thankfully my lava's inside, but it strains.
>
> —Aaren Yeatts Perry

The same thing can be done with a single body part for earlier grades when you are explaining the biological function of an organ like the esophagus. As they think and write, similes and metaphors will occur to the poets. Attaching these images to the organ's name will help students remember its function.

## I'M BIO-LOGICAL

Grades: 2-6

Cross-curricula: Science, English

Write a declarative poem celebrating the body's biological functions. Have a discussion about the functions of the human body. Using "I'm logical, I'm biological," as the chorus, students can write a rap poem in rhyming couplets about the importance of breathing, skin, blood circulation, sleeping, eating, sight, the nervous system, or musculature and physical exercise.

Bio-Logical poems can be applied to any curriculum area. Take grammar and parts of speech, for example. Have the students list all the parts of speech they know. Write a poem using a parallel opening to each line. In the poem, each part of the body becomes a part of speech and a part of the poem. "The hands of this poem are verbs, clapping, snapping, holding, squeezing. The head of this poem is an adjective, round as a pumpkin. This poem's thighs are nouns: tree and stilt. The shins of this poem are also nouns but long and proper like Mississippi and Monongahela." You may use this exercise as a grammar test for parts of speech by creating an animal or human figure or a varied landscape and writing the words *noun, adjective,* or *adverb* next to each object.

Have the students try to bring the poem to life rather than simply filling in the blanks. After the first draft, ask the poets to expand the poem by explaining what the hands are clapping about, and so on for each body part.

An ambitious poet could even use the persona technique again and describe a body made up of the elements of poetry: "A stomach full of metaphors with an indigestion of cats and dogs / My vertebrae are an acrostic with phrases of ribs. . . ." After reading and editing once, offer poets the same encouragement to rewrite and further develop the metaphors before going on to the next assignment.

A more coordinated effort can be attempted using, say, a science lesson on rain forests: "My body is a jungle. My toes are a rushing river always wiggling in my socks of moss and ferns. My hair is made of vines full of toucans. My back is an arch of palms that leads up to my head: a cluster of coconuts; branches my arms, branches my fingers. Leaves my skin. My skin, leaves." Give the poets time to rewrite and make the poems as complex as they want.

## NOTES

1. Jack Canfield and Harold Clive Wells, *100 Ways to Enhance Self-Concept in the Classroom* (Boston: Allyn and Bacon, 1994), p. 180.
2. Linda Noble Topf, *You Are Not Your Illness* (New York: Simon & Schuster, 1995).
3. Etheridge Knight, "He Sees through Stone," in *Born of a Woman* (Boston: Houghton Mifflin, 1980), p. 6.
4. William Stafford, "Right to Die," in S. Walker and R. Roffman, eds., *Life on the Line: Selections on Words and Healing* (Mobile, AL: Negative Capability Press, 1992), p. 51.
5. S. Walker and R. Roffman, eds., *Life on the Line: Selections on Words and Healing* (Mobile, AL: Negative Capability Press, 1992).
6. Pablo Neruda, "Walking Around," in Robert Bly, James Hillman, Michael Meade, eds., *The Rag and Bone Shop of the Heart* (New York: HarperCollins, 1992), p. 105.

7. Zora Neal Hurston, *Sanctified Church* (Berkeley, CA: Turtle Island Press, 1981).

8. Ibid., p. 19.

9. Topf, *You Are Not Your Illness.*

10. Koch, *Wishes, Lies, and Dreams*, p. 275.

# 5

# Music

Music is another important juncture where poetry and academic curricula meet. The poet can perform with musical instruments, or the poet can *be* the instruments. The ear, as I explain it to my elementary students, is a musical instrument. The vocal chords or "voice box" in the larynx are a musical instrument. Music is what happens when someone is reading a poem aloud and someone else is listening to it. The poet Etheridge Knight, explaining his tradition of "toasting" and "signifying," often said that poetry as a spoken art is a sacred trinity: "the poet, the poem, and the people." Like the musician with the instrument, the poet through the poem activates the listener, thereby creating a "communion."

*This Jazz*

It makes me feel like soft butter on a hot pancake.
Sometimes I feel happy.
Sometimes I feel sad.
Even sometimes I feel mad.
But this jazz
it makes me feel
like soft butter on a hot pancake.

—Ashley Hastings (Grade 4)

In introducing music and poetry I always discuss the word *muse*. I explain that it's O.K. to muse. And I tell classes that "the muse" is also a thing, similar to an idea, inspiration, or love. One can suddenly feel it (muse) for no apparent reason and one can practice it (musing). With older students, the image of the muse as a Cupid figure who travels around shooting people with arrows of love can lead to a discussion of the various deities and saints of communication: those mythological intermediators between the spirit and real world known as Hermes (Greek), Mercury (Roman), Anubis (Egyptian), Exu (Yoruban), and so on. Every culture has at least one.

For elementary students, I also explain that poetry is story leaning toward music. Poetry is what brings good stories to life, and it is what is inside of good song. Both need poetry. When you say a poem you're telling a story, but you're almost singing it—"singing a story." Then I ask why people sing, and a discussion begins about conveying thoughts and emotions. How do you feel when someone sings you a song? What types of things need a poem or song to be said in just the right way?

Memorization is inherent in song. Try to find someone who has never had a song "stuck in her head all day." The elements of music that lend themselves to memorization are also sitting right there in poetry and text: rhythm, rhyme, repetition, alliteration, syllabic meter. To prove this, simply try to memorize 10 lines of free-verse poetry and 10 lines of metered-verse poetry. The rhythmic will "stick" faster. And there are many, many different meters and rhythms. The North Indian classical music of the tabla drum, for example, is played to a 5-count, 19-count, sometimes 78-count rhythm! To help memorize these rhythms, tabla teachers sometimes use poetry. Musical words like, *ta*, *da*, *dit*, and *tak* are used like a song to express verbally a drum rhythm and teach music through math and poetry.

What is taught in a classroom that has no music and poetry will fall on deaf ears. Music and poetry open up the senses and give other important educational information a personal and memorable place to live.

Music and poetry are also similar in terms of discipline. In a public radio interview in 1995, Dave Brubeck, jazz pianist and composer of the famous composition "Take Five," said it was categorically true that all of his students for whom music study became a discipline showed dramatic academic improvement and consistently high academic scores.

It is true of any endeavor that, when it is practiced regularly, one's other activities and quality of life improve. Goethe said, ". . . the moment one definitely commits oneself, then Providence moves too."[1] Poetry is no exception.

*Music*

This music sounds like
bananas smashing
like beans shaking,
like my mother chopping chicken
on the fourth of July.

—Kathleen Rodriquez (Grade 3)

## MUSIC

Grades: 3–6

Cross-curricula: English, Art

Preactivity Class Reading: "Funk Lore" by Amiri Baraka,[2] "Beat! Beat! Drums!" by Walt Whitman [3]

Bring in albums or tapes of jazz music. Instrumentals containing bass, piano, drum, or saxophone solos can be inspirational. You will already know well the type of music that is popular in your class. This is a time to challenge students with other music that is appealing in new and different ways.

**1.** At first, just have students listen and write single words or phrases that come to mind to describe the music. If they are prolific, they can put these together in their own poems.

**2.** If the words are not flowing that day, write what words they do have on the board and create a group Renga in which you use a simile to describe what different parts of the music are "like or as."

A diamante poem can contrast the two different instruments within a musical duet.

**3.** Ask students to think in a certain direction about musical perception. How would the music feel if it were a thing you could hold or a living entity coming toward you? "We tried to hold jazz/but it dripped [where?] hot and gooey, dough-like,/squealing at us like a whale [why?]/then it popped and flooded the school [with what?]/We picked some up and fell asleep on it [dreaming?]/The ending was a pillow of zzz's/until bottles and windows broke and woke us."

Or what would it look like all together if it were an animal or living thing. Have each student write what and who they are when they are the music:

> I am a twenty-legged elephant
> with sharp trunks and beaks
> flattening ears with boomeranging car horns. . . .

Keep asking students to deepen their ideas as with the above interspersed questions.

**4.** Another approach is to ask students to pick an instrument they can identify within the recording. Ask them to imagine that they know that instrument's language. Have them say in a poem what the instrument was saying in its solo. You can find a good guitar, flute, sax, piano, bass, percussion, or drum solo on a jazz or rock album for this.

**5.** Kenneth Koch suggested that concept poems such as "I Wish" and "I Used to Be / But Now I Am" might work better when writing poems to music. But he also encouraged his students to allow the music to influence the type of poem they wrote. "I told them to write whatever the music made them think of—their poem could be a story, a dream, description of a scene, whatever they wanted."[4]

## MUSICAL IMAGERY

Grades: 4–6

Cross-curricula: Social Studies

Using the same steps and tools as in the previous exercise, have the students describe the music you are listening to as if they were looking at a painting. What is in the background? What is in the foreground? What colors does each instrument evoke? What textures or patterns are they making? How big is it, and what feeling does it give the people who are looking at it? Who is painting it and in what setting? Is it still being painted or is it already in an exhibit? Where is that exhibit? This music makes me see . . .

Try to inspire the use of more challenging descriptive words. This is a good opportunity for writers to use terms such as *unity* and *rhythm*. By third or fourth grade they should be able to access and use a poetic vocabulary full of words like *tempo, tone, pitch, harmony, melody, loud, soft, driving, galloping*. The common language of music and poetry lends itself to discovery. The musical concepts of *tempo change, syllable, phrase, verse, chorus,* and *meter* appear in poetry.

Does the idiom of music you are listening to evoke certain overall images? If it is folk music, what scene does that musical style and name awareness bring to mind for the students? If it is jazz? Is it an instrument they are hearing for the first time, such as an Australian *dijerydoo*, a Mexican rain stick, or a Caribbean conch shell or steel drum? Is it a real acoustical instrument? Or is it an electronic instrument that is re-creating the original sound? Is it using air, percussion, vibration?

This could be a chance to talk about cultural stereotypes versus music as a universal language and cultural border crosser. Some lute-like stringed instruments in Africa, Asia, and the Middle East sound a lot like an Appalachian banjo. Where is the music being played? On the porch of a muddy house in Hazard County, Tennessee? In the White House, the Taj Mahal, a desert canyon, the Alps, a cave? Who is playing it? And what is the music causing its listeners to do?

*"When the mode of music changes, the walls of the city shake."*—Plato

## STRIKE UP THE BAND

Grades: 1–6

Preactivity Class Reading: "Jazz Fantasia" by Carl Sandburg[5]

Live musicians in the classroom always create a cathartic experience for elementary students. Whether it is a solo percussionist, a wind instrumentalist, or a guitarist, a good poet/musician can provide the ultimate connection between the visceral, rhythmic voicing of poetry and the intelligible writing of poetry on the page.

If you are able to teach your class a simple rhythm or repetitive phrase on a drum or any kind of portable instrument, it may be possible to arrange some musical accompaniment for your poets. I have done this several times using cassette tapes of hip-hop or rap rhythms that have no lyrics. I have used a conga drum as the background rhythm for a group heroes rap poem (see the Social Studies chapter). In lieu of instruments, hand clapping, toe tapping, and finger snapping are certainly accessible and promote group coordination and listening.

Slippery Man took my phone
Slippery Man took my phone
Greased up his arm and stole that
  talk box from my happy home

Now the nights are quiet
Can't hear your sweet voice calling me
Said the nights are so quiet
Can't hear your sweet voice calling me
A telephone that walks can't ring
just dial me up and you will see

He took my shoes, my wallet, my watch,
like this was where he shops
But when that bad guy took my phone
I couldn't even call the cops
Oh, Mr. Slippery, sure thinks he is wise
Next time he'll get a poem full of knuckles
right between his very eyes

—**Aaren Yeatts Perry**

## BLUES POEMS

Grades: 3–6

Cross-curricula: Health, Human Values

The blues is probably more pervasive in American music and literature than any other musical genre. It inspired the development of rock, pop, jazz, gospel, and some folk music. It is popular in Europe, Asia, and Africa. And, with just three chords and twelve bars, it is one of the simplest yet most touching musical forms.

Blues lyrics are a form of poetry. Like dramatic tragedy on the stage, the blues often deals with love and loss. But it can treat a limitless array of problems with every emotion from high humor to deep sadness.

If you cannot find a blues musician to come to your classroom to talk about blues writing, there are thousands of blues recordings that are appropriate for the elementary grades. Taj Majal is one of many blues artists who have widely available children's recordings. Much of his work is relatively light-hearted blues. Langston Hughes's collections of poetry contain some of the most accessible, well-written blues poetry. He wrote about some of the most difficult issues facing humanity.

Whatever author you choose to read with your class, you will find one of a few different formulas used. Rhyming couplets in *a-b-a-b* form are the most popular. Another common form is a repetition lament, which repeats the first line twice, followed by a third chorus or punch line. The third line can either rhyme with the first two (as in the poem above), rhyme with the punch line of the next stanza, or not rhyme with anything.

**1.** Conduct a blues brainstorming discussion in which you ask the class to give you a list of things that give them the blues. As you make the list, try to get students to name the type of blues they get using compound words. Your brainstorming list may include issues such as baby siblings (screaming sister blues), money or allowance (poor poet blues), food (empty lunch box or boring lunch blues), parents, toys (broken toy blues), bullies (big bad boy blues), the weather (floodwater blues), or even homework and school (bad grade blues). Using such compound words, you can name the type of blues these things cause you.

**2.** After discussing where the blues comes from, suggest that one good way to battle the blues is by writing the blues! The first approach is to write two to four blues rhymes aimed at one of the problems. Describe how bad it is using similes: "Baby sister screams so loud, sounds like someone dying to me. She takes one drink of milk and she's quiet as could be." Some blues lyrics resolve how they will fix the problem; others say things are too bad to fix.

**3.** You could open a line with an exclamatory ("Hey, money!") or a conciliatory ("Please, money . . .") tone. Ask the problem causer to solve the problem for you, or ask it to stop. Either way, the blues poem should describe what kind of pain the author is feeling. Simile ("You make me feel down like . . .") and metaphor ("I'm broke. I'm a broken bank.") to the rescue.

**4.** The second approach is to write a blues poem directed at a friend or relative asking for understanding about the problem. For example, another stanza of the Slippery Man Blues (based on a Southern folk character) changes audience and goes, "Slippery Man gonna get you too. Slippery Man gonna get you too. Don't let your loved one sleep by the window, even if your loved one's true."

When you have a completed set of blues lines, ask students for a title. Sometimes the title will have been the inspiration for the song. Have them write another set. Ask for someone who can sing one of the poems in a blues melody.

*Blues*

Blues are like a sadness
as blues rise from Black people's
souls as a man just told me
what the blues are—and as a
jazz tune it comes from the heart
as I hear the beauty
of the culture of jazz.

—Billy Nenadich (Grade 4)

## THE WORDS NOISES SAY

Grades: 1–6

This is about the words inside sounds. In the "Noises" section of his book *Wishes, Lies, and Dreams,*[6] Kenneth Koch explains that he asked the students to do two different things with sound: "make sound comparisons (say what sounds like what), and write whole lines that imitated a particular sound ('The clink was like a drink of pink water')." Learning about the use of sound in poetry helps expand the students' repertoire of poetic tools.

**1.** Koch says he asked grades 1 through 3 "for sound comparisons and for how things 'went.' " "The moose went 'whoooonk.' " Fourth through sixth graders can be asked to make this same type of sound comparison. Older students should be challenged to make more complex comparisons. They are capable of making sound comparisons and imitations throughout a whole stanza or poem. Words that are newly invented in this process can be entered into the class dictionary of invented words.

**2.** After the initial discussion with the class, Koch asked the students to close their eyes as he made the sound of his hand smacking a book over and over again. He then asked them to "try to hear a word in the noise. . . . Once they were thinking this way about sounds I had them write the poems." Students may want to hear some of the sounds again, but once they have their lists of words, encourage them to write.

**3.** Present some sounds that speak, such as water dripping or running onto various hollow or rough surfaces; moving saws with varying-sized teeth slowly or quickly through cardboard, wood, metal, or plastic; zipping zippers in various sizes of garments; a squeaky door; quickly or slowly ripping various thicknesses of paper or cardboard; scooting a chair; tossing empty plastic jugs of various sizes and shapes down the hallway floors; breaking various sizes of glasses and bottles in a deep cardboard box; dropping a cloth bag full of marbles, coins, or chains onto a hard surface; dropping a big wad of keys onto the floor; hitting a chair, desk, wall, or book with a ruler, book, or hand; shaking a penny in a glass jar, two pennies, three washers; tubular chimes; rain on various objects; traffic; a conch shell!

## WORD MUSIC: ALLITERATION

Grades: 1–3

Students can invent new words by interpreting the sounds of the natural and machine world.

**1.** Still using the basic *goes* form, try building a combination of three descriptive alliterations that describe an object's noise-making both musically and objectively. "Swimmy, swishy, swasher goes the dish washer."

**2.** The third descriptive alliteration should rhyme with the name of the object: "Skid, sklank, skates go the dinner plates." "Wind, whine, whams. The washer door slams!"

**3.** Once you have a chalkboard full of these combinations, you can read them through, aloud with the students, while keeping time by clapping. The rules should be clear enough from the group samples for the writing students to create a few on their own.

## THERE'S A TIME AND A PLACE

Grades: 1–6

Other sounds that are fresh and clear in students' minds include noises from various rooms in their homes, noises that their parents or siblings make, noises at the zoo, noises from their neighborhoods, noises at night or in the daytime, noises at their parent's job. Except for outer space, there is noplace that has no sound. Is there a time during which there is no sound?

**1.** As a prewriting exercise ask students for 10 different times of the day, including night, dawn, rush hour, midnight, dusk, and so on.

**2.** After writing these on the board (or having students write them individually on their papers), ask them for 10 different places that they know or love. Try to get a diverse list of places. Ask what sounds are heard in those places at those times.

**3.** Once these are written, add three more times on the opposite side of the clock and ask what sounds are heard at those times.

**4.** Now ask individual students to do the same with some places and times that are special to them because of the sounds that are heard.

**5.** Add a synesthesia step in which the poets write what it looks, smells, tastes, and feels like when that sound is heard.

*Paper Boy (Excerpt)*

Deep in the moldy hush of the still life pre-dawn
when even the sleepless have fallen asleep,
when the misty smells of rotten rugs catch fire
in distant train moans, I bring your horoscope,
rubberband it to your want ads and vacancies
and slam it against your storm door with a bang
that throws on lights, fries bacon and eggs . . .

—Aaren Yeatts Perry

## MOVEMENT AND POETRY

Grades: 1–6

Words, like any sound vibration, can cause the human body to want to move, tap toes, shake heads, shout out, or even dance. I have worked in several programs where students were able to bring their poems to a movement specialist or dance choreographer and develop a whole dance program based on their poetry.

The students can either dance to their own poems while a dramatic reading is going on, or read their own work while trained dancers perform. Either way, the process of artists working together in collaboration helps deepen their understanding of the power of words and the relationship of poetry to other disciplines.

With both movement and visiting musicians, there may be a group of local performers who will come to your school for an assembly or to work with students in separate classes. In many cases the group will be able to conduct similar workshops in which the writing process is done in teams. Similar assignments are made, but more than one adult circulates and works more closely with each group of writing students. With the right planning, this type of team teaching can be done with parents, community representatives, local artists, and student teachers. Then the pieces are put together in a performance. A similar approach is used by the Banner Project in Pennsylvania. "Like the persistent turtle," says the Banner Project, "one teacher can affect a group of children and send a ripple of change throughout the school."[7]

Try a simple movement exercise in which you read to the class a dramatic poem with intense emphases or tempo variations. After they have listened to it once, ask the class if they saw or felt any movements that they would like to try. As examples of movement phrases emerge, split the class up into small groups who can execute the movements. Have a couple of groups of readers work with a couple of groups of movers. Repeat and combine different moves, extending them into the whole body as space allows.

When the class has "interpreted" the whole poem, have the groups rehearse and then perform it as a stretch or warm-up exercise during bad weather, when students can't go outside.

## CHORAL READING

Grades: 1–6

Teachers in the early grades can orchestrate a choral reading of a group poem written on the board. Assign small groups different parts of a poem and have them repeat their part until they have it memorized. The other groups can be added as you explain how the parts work together.

In grades 3 through 6 students can work in small groups to orchestrate choral arrangements of poems they have written. Some of the poetry-writing exercises in this book lend themselves to this type of reading. Students can create soundscapes, voice percussions, "human beat boxes," or background scat rhythms. They can alternate reading lines or stanzas in a poem that requires soft/loud, fast/slow, or high/low voices. Poems with a common chorus, ballads, and parallel poems with repeated lines work well.

Fifth graders have written science and social studies lessons into choral readings. One eighth-grade physical education class wrote soccer rules in a choral reading format.[8]

The more technical and poetic the language is, the more unique it will sound when arranged. Your daily class schedule with descriptive statements from each period added in would be an interesting beginning. Try parts to a bicycle or directions to and from a specific location using the names of streets in your neighborhood.

**1.** Go to your Group Poems Book and select any poem written by your class. Read through it and refamiliarize yourself with it.

**2.** Make copies of the poem and have the class read it together.

**3.** Using rows of students or small groups scattered throughout the classroom, assign numbers or letters to each "voice group." Have students mark their part of the poem with their group number. You could begin by simply splitting up the lines of a poem sequentially, as with any group reading assignment in which you go around the room giving each student an opportunity to read part of a story or poem.

**4.** When the groups know who they are and are aware of timing, begin to experiment with pitch and tone (voice quality), decibel modulation (loudness or softness), timing, and phrasing. For example, you can assign one group to repeat in either a monotone or gradually higher voices a key phrase, refrain, or chorus in a poem, while the rest of the students read the rest of the poem over this background chorus.

**5.** Another approach is to say a poem in choral rounds. Start by having students sing any rounds song, from "Row, Row, Row Your Boat," to "The Battle Hymn of the Republic." Any song or poem that uses repetition at the beginning or within it will support a good rounds reading. For a poem to work in rounds, the group must agree on a rhythm and timing for the poem so that each group knows when to join in.

**6.** Explore the possibilities of assigning the words from any curriculum-related prewriting or brainstorming list to be spoken with varied phrasing. In this activity one group sustains an arc of sound containing the vowel in a word—*clouds*, for example. During this arc of sound, another choral group can say another phrase made up of words dealing with the same science lesson on weather: ". . . gather when weather gets madder at water and scatters it to the skyyyyyyyyyyy." When both of those groups finish at the exact same time, third group can finish the sentence with another phrase like, ". . . by heating?" A fourth group can add the answer, "Yes, or by coooooooling it." These word songs can help students understand group timing, coordination, and pronunciation; and they provide an opportunity for dramatization.

## CHORAL RAP BAND

Grades: 3–6

Another approach to musical and choral poetry is the rap poem. Some forms of hip-hop and rap poetry are composed of free verse or rhyme schemes that are improvised around a complex interaction with the rhythm. In lieu of this, you can begin with a simple rhyming couplet and build from there. What follows is a musical exercise to be combined with or used as a musical accompaniment to the suggested rap poem (see the Group Heroes rap poem in the Social Studies chapter) or any poetry reading.

**1.** See if you can orchestrate the different pieces of a musical rap band. First ask the class if there is anyone who can imitate a musical instrument or be a "human beat box." This begins to remove the inhibitions of what will be a public display of silly mouth noises, and it will give you a sense, if you don't know already, of how musically skilled your class is.

**2.** Bring in a recording of a blank rap track (the music with no lyrics). Begin by playing it through and asking students to identify the different instruments. The best selection is one that begins with a single instrument and then builds, one instrument at a time.

**3.** Rewind to the beginning and start with the drums. Ask everyone wearing a certain color, or everyone from your reading group "A," for example, to repeat a simple but clear drum beat. What letters and mouth shapes are used? How much force is required? Experiment with mouth shapes and sound until your drum group is convincing.

**4.** Without accompaniment, ask group "B" to imitate the bass and follow the bass line through the first few measures of the song. Make sure it is a sound that can work with the drums and that the other instruments can follow. Do this with each instrument separately until all instruments have been re-created with your students' voices.

**5.** Eventually, have the musical instruments modulate their volume to a quieter level so that individual students can say their poems with the band as a musical background.

## NOTES

1. Goethe, "Commitment," in Robert Bly, James Hillman, and Michael Meade, eds., *The Rag and Bone Shop of the Heart* (New York: HarperCollins, 1992), p. 235.

2. Imamu Amiri Baraka, "Funk Lore," in Maria Mazziotti Gillan and Jennifer Gillan, eds., *Unsettling America* (New York: Penguin Books, 1994) p. 156.

3. Walt Whitman, "Beat! Beat! Drums!" in Alexander W. Allison et al., eds., *The Norton Anthology of Poetry Revised* (New York: W. W. Norton, 1975), p. 822.

4. Kenneth Koch, *Wishes, Lies, and Dreams* (New York: Harper & Row, Publishers, 1970), p. 245.

5. Carl Sandburg, "Jazz Fantasia," in *Harvest Poems 1910–1960* (New York: Harcourt, Brace and World, 1960), p. 59.
6. Koch, *Wishes, Lies, and Dreams*, p. 126.
7. The Banner Project, *Building a Rainbow* (Phoenixville, PA: The Banner Project, 1994), p. ii.
8. J. McCauley and D. McCauley, "Using Choral Reading to Promote Language Learning for ESL Students," *The Reading Teacher* 45(7), 1992, pp. 526–533.

# ▶ 6

# Science

Poetry and science are old friends. From Pythagoras to Prometheus, from Jason to Magellan, scientific discovery has been recognized, memorialized, and glorified by poets. The life, earth, physical, and mechanical sciences all contain language that is naturally poetic in that they combine and describe concepts that everyday speech does not usually combine and describe.

Poetry is, in a general sense, nature writing. Like science, it seeks to explain the essential nature of things. Nature is the subject of much great poetry as a metaphor for humanity's imperfection and greatness and as a constant reminder that we are part of nature, and smaller than the universe.

To write poetry requires a great knowledge of many things, not the least of which are scientific concepts. The proverbial journey of the poet is to place himself in and become nature, and then return to tell of the wilderness.

The concepts of elementary science are just as poetic as those of advanced science. This chapter contains writing exercises that reflect and explore those concepts. Here are writing exercises related to math, time, measurement, location, transportation, architecture, seeds, food, pollution, stages of development, animals, sensation, seasons, space, geology, and the environment.

## I WISH I WAS AN ANIMAL

Grades: 1–3

The ever-popular "I Wish" poems are a great match for science content. They require the writer to use science facts to convince the reader of the urgency and verity of the wish. For first grade you can conduct this activity as a group and take answers from all students. For writing students you can do a few together, then assign solo writing.

**1.** Start a group writing activity by asking the younger students if they have ever been another animal or wanted to be. Everyone likes to pretend to be his favorite animal. What animals do your students know about? Are you introducing new ones?

**2.** Once you get a list of animals written on the board that the students wish to be, go back over it and, one at a time, write a line for each animal. Ask the students to explain their animals: What type of bird, caged or wild? What do you do all day? Where do you live? What do you eat and how do you play? Are you a hungry or mean or quiet or lurking or friendly one? How big? Describe your color and markings, the feel of your skin, the look in your eyes, your favorite food, your dreams.

**3.** After the first few lines of description, ask for a last line that says "so that I could . . ." What special things could you *do* if you were that boa? What would you want to do?

Those students who for some reason don't want to be an animal in this context may respond better to the question of "I want to be a cougar when . . ."; "I could really use the power and size of being an elephant when I . . ."

The lines can rhyme or can all be the same length so that the students can clap along when you read it back together. Or the poem can have no restrictions and will still work well.

**4.** When you have a paragraph written on the board for a few of the animals, tell the older students to write about the animals they want to be.

*"The deep things in science are not found because they are useful. They are found because it is possible to find them."*
—Robert Oppenheimer[1]

## SEEDS POEMS

Grades: 2–4

When discussing plants, growth, and seed properties, and after students can identify seeds such as pea, clover, grass, pumpkin, and sunflower, try a poetry-writing exercise about imaginary plants to explore the growth stages.

**1.** On the board or on a worksheet, draw three or four different types of seeds. Next to the seed write a description of its life cycle in the first person. "I emerge as a furry orange flower in fall and crawl across the dirt on a vine."

**2.** Have students help you compose a riddle-like description of who you are and what you do when you grow. "I sit there soaking up the autumn colors until I am as fat and full and orange as a harvest moon rising. It sometimes takes three children to carry me. They carve me into mean monsters and light me up. Really I just want to be a nice pie with whipped cream."

**3.** Bring in a bag of seeds mixed with tiny objects similar in size and shape to seeds: nuts, bolts, pieces of candy corn, small buttons, fake gems, cereal, pebbles, crayon pieces, rings, keys, an eraser tip.

Plant the "seeds" in the palms of each student's hands individually so that only the individual can see what it is.

**4.** Ask students to write as many lines as they can, predicting what the imaginary plant will look like when it sprouts. "The first thing you will see when I sprout will be a wool collar." or "After my arms are fully grown I will produce three big brown button down fruit on the front of my trunk. I am the one with no zipper, but I will grow a lined hood. I usually appear in late fall and go back into mothballs around spring."

What will grow out of it when it is full grown? What fruit or seeds will it produce? Write the words, shapes, sizes, colors, textures, and material on the board. Encourage students to include as many descriptive words as possible. Later, titles can be added like "The Mysterious Winter Coat Plant."

## POLLUTION POEMS

Grades: 1–6

The poetic device of persona can enable a student to inform, describe, and persuade an audience about pollution. By becoming either a pollutant or a polluted element, as with the "conversations" poems, the writer can describe in the first person the senses and circumstances of being polluted. Another use of persona is an "I Used to Be/But Now I Am" poem, written in a warning, fury, or parallel structure to indicate nature's tendency to rejuvenate itself.

Students should be encouraged to use alliteration and onomatopoeia to illustrate the sounds of the element they choose to inhabit. Sixth graders reading texts about the Environmental Protection Agency's top 10 clean-up sites or books such as Rachel Carson's *Silent Spring* can decide whether environmental conditions are improving or worsening during their lifetimes.

**1.** Brainstorm a list of natural systems and elements that can be polluted. With what are they polluted? How are humans and animals affected?

**2.** Have the class help you write a short poem on the board in which you are either a pollutant or polluted natural element. Explain that you want the poem to speak in the first-person voice of the element.

**3.** Instruct all students to make the same choices for their poems. Have them list the two most polluted environments they know of. How did they get this way? What people and animals are affected by this? Focus on being and speaking as the element they chose: Is the poet/voice the victim or cause of pollution? What does the future hold for you as a pollutant or as a polluted ecosystem?

*I Am Pollution*

I am black smoke filling the skies.
I leap out of chimneys like black panthers. . . .

—Ricky Ingram

## EARTH DAY POEMS

Grades: 3–6

You may want to try a similar chain reaction poem describing in a lyrical way how a healthy and normally functioning ecosystem interacts. When the class has a studied grasp of ecosystems, they can write a group "chain reaction" or "food chain" poem.

**1.** First discuss a specific ecosystem that has been polluted, and review all the affected inhabitants.
**2.** A poem can begin with the first student writing a rhyming stanza from the perspective of the smallest organism affected, then passing it on to the second student. The second writer describes in a rhyming stanza how life is different for the second largest organism now that the smallest is polluted, and so on up the chain.
**3.** The exercise can utilize facts from science lessons on animals that are endangered or extinct. Or it can be used as an activity around a discussion of recycling.

A commandment poem can be written from the perspective of one of the natural environments affected by pollution. In such a poem, the revolt of the natural element takes the form of commanding humanity to stop polluting—or says that it's already too late! For example, a spring can speak to a poet about being silenced in a poem titled "Still Silent." Or a spring can talk about getting its voice back and flowing clearly again in "Now I Can Tell You."

Coordinate this writing exercise with annual Earth Day in April or with other environmental activities such as neighborhood clean-up.

*The Way I Used to Be*

I was air as clean as a sunny day
until pollution came my way
and they came to destroy the world
so it would be polluted instead of a clean place.
I had to fight back so I went all over the lands
and got some of my clean family and came back.
This went on for a month until the end
and I was the only one living
and my family got polluted and died of being sick.
I had some pollution in me but still lived
and I will never forget how I used to be.
Clean, clean, clean as a sunny day.

—Mozell Williams (Grade 3)

## FOOD CHAIN

Grades: 2–5

**1.** Begin by discussing some of the students' favorite foods. Where do they come from? What animals? What plants? Try to take this discussion down the food chain to the smallest organism your class can conceptualize. Use this as an opportunity to discuss the concept of limited resources, the size of our planet, and the interdependence of elements and resources.

**2.** Now they can write their way back up the food chain using an "I Used to Be / But I Was Eaten by" poem. "I used to be soil/corn/corn meal/tortilla . . ." "I used to be a bug . . ." What kind of bug? "But I was eaten by a snake/the snake by a coyote/the coyote by a bear."

**3.** Some students may go quickly from smallest to largest. For example, "I used to be little green plankton / floating freely in the sea/ but I was eaten by a whale who didn't see me." Try to get them to think of animals of every size and make the chain as long as possible.

**4.** When they edit, can they add another line to each chain link saying how they were living at each stage? What they were doing when they were eaten? How did they look? Where did they live?

## BORN FREE

Grades: 1–3

Persona can also be used to explain in a poetic way a child's understanding of the phenomenon of reproduction and metamorphosis.

**1.** In science units where you are discussing the birth process and developmental stages, ask for some examples of babies: puppies, kittens, foals (baby horses), fawns, cubs, chicks.

**2.** Write a group poem in which the class agrees to be a group of one of these kinds of animals. Ask them as many questions as you have time to discuss and write on the board with them.

**3.** Question and lead students to explain in the poem the stages of development that they know. Were they born in the wild or in captivity? Did another type of animal try to prey on them when they were infants? What are the sounds they make when they are happy, angry, hungry, sleepy? What do the like to eat? "Soon we will be . . ."—the equivalent of child, toddler, teenager, adult? What will they do to survive when they become adults? How many offspring will there be if each of the students has as many as the number of their class? What can they do to live together without overcrowding?

## TRANSFORMATION: USED TO BE/BUT NOW

Grades: 2–6

Cross-curricula: Social Studies

Pre-Activity Class Reading: Frank O'Hara's "Autobiographia Literaria"[2]

This exercise is useful for writing poems of comparison and contrast. It is a good way to study sequence and progression and to develop through writing a sense of passage of time and interconnectedness.

A structured verse format could use the simple A-B-A-B rhyming couplet: "I used to be a seed/but now I am a tree/growing is a need/but soon I'll outgrow me!"

A free-verse poem can take on many dimensions. If the class has studied water or weather in science classes, you can ask the students to write a poem starting with "I used to be a drop of water / now I am . . ." Or they can explore the different stages of fire by starting with a spark. After any line, the poem can go into detail about what it's like to have turned from a spark or a match into a blazing forest fire or the sun!

Within this simple structure, the writer has a lot more room to explore the depths of the imagination for description, feeling, and lyrical choices.

## MATH HOUSE POEMS

Grades: 3–6

As a warm-up exercise that reviews placement and sequence, have students close their eyes and count how many rooms are in their house. Did they include the closets, cabinets, and bathrooms? The attic and basement? Are poems hidden in their house? Ask if anyone can tell you exactly how many doors.

**1.** Now ask them to close their eyes and go back through the house beginning with the front door and counting in sequence or places: first, second, third.

**2.** When the counting stops, explain that they will go back again and describe each door by saying what the door looks like (recommend shapes, comparisons), what it says (noises and words), what it always does (verbs: *guards, hides, protects, keeps*), or what it would rather be doing. Ask if they can describe each door in their house using only the number.

> The first one is old, bold, moldy, big knocker, no number.
> The second pristine, squeaky clean, leans to kiss passersby,
> shines.
> The third is a swinger, sings, "soup'son, soup'son, soup'son."
> The fourth always slams, looks at Grams, says, "Aw, come on!"
> The last is small, austere, remembers coal, keeps out dark, no
> fear.
>
> —Aaren Yeatts Perry

## ILLOGICAL NUMBERS POEMS

Grades: 4–6

Using simple if/then algebraic equations with numbers and words, poems can be written in addition, subtraction, division, and multiplication language that are fun and that may contain meaningful statements about a student's life.

**1.** Begin by making a list of numbers on the board around a theme: qualities of objects or concepts from an English, social studies, or science lesson, zoo trip, home and family, school.

**2.** Ask students how many there are of each item, for example, in their home: four plates, six pots and three pans, two dogs, five fish, two brothers, one sister, two bedrooms, one fish tank, seven piles of paper, and so on.

**3.** With this list, you can ask students to help you create imaginary mathematical equations that are poetic and funny. Help them with the poetic and nonnumerical sum of their equations in a couple of trial runs on the board.

If I added all my grandparents
with my brothers, sister and parents
we would have a house of twelve
empty plates and a clean table.
We would soon be zero from hunger.
If I subtracted the pets
we would still be hungry . . .

—Group Sample (Grades 2 and 3)

For higher grades, the same thing can be done with division and multiplication:

The ball court divided by recess
equals two mean half-court games
with thirty fouls and jump balls.
One-third of the upper school
times Mr. Mann's boom box
plus one-twelfth of my rap tape
equals a private room on a floor
in the sky with zero office
and zero homework.

—Group Sample Poem (Grades 2 and 3)

## NUMBERS METAPHOR POEMS

Grades: 1–3

Pre-Activity Class Reading: "Numbers Man" and "Arithmetic" in Carl Sandburg's *Harvest Poems 1910–1960*[3]

This exercise is a simple metaphor-maker using numbers. Saying the name of a number can evoke many images.

**1.** Begin with single-digit numbers. Explain that for each number you say the name of, you would like a student to tell you the name of an object that it brings to mind. There are not many things of which only one exists: the sun, the sky, and so on. But there may be plenty of singular things in a child's eyes. Try to steer students away from the "Twelve Days of Christmas" or other number metaphor poems and songs.

**2.** Begin with one and count upwards. Follow each number with *is*. "Seven is the number on my jersey, my age." "Eight is bedtime, story time, the pool ball winner." "Nine is my cat." Do a couple of two-digit numbers as well. "Eleven is the store sign on Fourth Street glowing at night." "Twenty-two is a flock of geese above honking." See how many references to recent lessons you can work into the poem.

**3.** For each number you may get a single word: "Nine is my cat." Draw out a longer line by asking, "Your cat doing what? What does she look like when she's doing that?"

**4.** For a more focused poem, conduct the exercise in a content area: farm numbers, ocean numbers, forest numbers, pioneer and settlers numbers.

## IN A HEARTBEAT

Grades: 3–6

Cross-curricula: Health

You only have a certain number of heartbeats in your life. How will you divide them up? Create fractions and tell what percentage you will use on each thing in your life. How many on yourself, on the people you love, on playing with animals, alone with nature, working, studying? Be as specific as possible.

You can easily write a love poem in a tanka, rengu, or haiku explaining how many of your heartbeats you'd spend on yourself, or on the people you love. Doing what together?

## LOCATION RIDDLE

Grades: 2–6

This is a kind of "Riddley-Riddley-Ree, I See Something You Don't See" writing exercise. The intention is to say what something is, not by naming it but by describing where it is in relation to other objects. If students can clearly describe an object's position, other students will be able to tell what it is.

**1.** First, list all the prepositions your class knows: *above, on, over, under, beneath, below, beside, between, beyond, through, at, in, inside, next to, before, behind.* Play a quick warm-up game of "Riddley-Riddley-Ree, I See Something You Don't See" in the classroom using two prepositions for each object. One at a time, a student chooses an object while classmates raise their hands and guess.

**2.** Have a discussion in which you talk about the natural objects your class has been studying: lights/electricity, plants/terrarium, animals, solids, gases, liquids. List some specific examples of each. Make a list long enough that it's not easy to guess which one a student will be describing.

**3.** Each grade will have a progressively larger repertoire of position words. Third graders, for example, should have access to words indicative of distance and direction: *very far, to the left of, to the right of, right behind, far above.*

**4.** Have students come up to the board one by one and pick an object. Have them tell you in the first person what they are and where they are located. When they have thought about its position and are ready to tell, have them either shut their eyes and picture the classroom object that they are, or turn their back to the class and look at the word on the board (if it is one of the discussion selections). Each line should begin with "I am . . ." plus the preposition. Have each of them use as many words from the list of prepositions as possible to describe the location of the object.

**5.** As students explain their positions you can have a scribe or student-teacher write them down or write them on the board. If they run out of prepositions, help them by suggesting others.

Whether the list is 3 lines long or 15, older students can then take the list and edit more description into it. Between the lines, a poet can add a word or phrase describing the texture, odor, color, sound, shape, size, and purpose of the objects involved.

Crow is whistling for a cab of wind home.
But steam wants a ride up to sky's big dome.
Steam laughs, takes the bus of heat waves,
Then pays with the money she saves
For the poor river to take a boat of land.
Everyone needs a ride.
Every grain of sand.

—Aaren Yeatts Perry

## TRANSPORTATION POEMS

Grades: 2–6

If your class is ready to write or scribe together a poem about transportation, take the list from the preceding exercise and add a second stanza to each poem in which the object that has been located and described decides that it wants to move.

**1.** How would your students describe the type of transportation their objects use to move from one place to another? Their objects may be made to move (horses, birds, wind), or they may seem impervious to movement. Where does the object want to go? Is it because of a cycle, a season, or a migration? As every living animal species has its own form of motion and transportation, so do inanimate objects. Ask students to use action words to describe the movement of a snail, a clam, a starfish, a crow, a dog, steam, fire, electricity, water, a stone, a leaf, a seed, or any other organism or object.

**2.** If the object described is a stone or a plant, and needs some help, who or what does it call (weather and other forces of nature) to assist it in its move? Does time still matter in its journey? Is it slow or fast or some other word? Have students list some action words that describe the transportation of their object and some of the ways it gets help. Describe the place where they are going, again using more prepositions.

**3.** Now have them write out a stanza about the object moving, using the prewriting information they have listed. When the second stanza is finished and students have described the process of transportation, have them read back over it and see if they want to add or take away anything.

A title can be pulled out of the writing. It still does not have to say the name of the object.

As with all poetry exercises, you can use the subject matter either as a way of introducing a content topic and beginning discussion, or as a way of testing and using that information.

*Leaf*

Beneath the sun and the moon
    Under feathered friends flying fast
Above picnickers and trashcans
    Hanging from a wooden pole
Outside a second story window
    Filled with sappy sugar
Between a spiderweb and bird's nest
    Shading over bugs like a green parasol
Up, over, and out like them I want to fly

Oh, wind who waves back at me everyday
from behind the steering wheel
of your giant airplane, take me
down fast and furious in the fall

Towards that army with rakes
    Bagging and burning, I'll lie
On the soft sofa of grass
    Dropping these seeds then wrinkling

Under a blanket of sky
    Shivering at the steel broom of autumn
In a pile of others like me
    Screaming our unread poems in the fire

—Aaren Yeatts Perry

Another type of transportation poem is, of course, about human transportation.

Here students can write a story poem detailing all the types of transportation on which they've traveled. Have them include as much information as they can about speed, distance, safety, landscape, purpose of trip, type of propulsion, and source of the energy that provides that propulsion.

Prolific and imaginative students can be asked to write a poetic travelogue recording a trip around the world in the year 2099. What are the new forms of transportation? The new names? How do they work?

Finally, a persona poem in which the poet becomes the mode of transportation can be fun. Ask the students to pick their favorite kind of transportation. Where do they go? With whom? How are they better than other forms of transportation for users? What do they sound and look like? What parts do they need? How are they kept? How do they move? Flashy, squeaky, quietly, loudly? What fuels are used? Do they use a fuel that is limited or limitless?

## PLAYING WITH YOUR FOOD

Grades: 1–4

Cross-curricula: Health

Food poems are good sources of writing inspiration, especially for the younger grades. Start by closing the eyes of just one student at a time.

**1.** Give the child one marshmallow (or peanut, gumdrop, orange slice, popcorn, spaghetti noodle, corn kernel, etc.).

**2.** Have the child give you words that describe the tastes, sensations, smells, memories, or feelings evoked by the food—anything but the appearance or name of the food. Do this verbally with a few individuals as an exercise toward writing the description of the food.

**3.** Then pass out an interesting food that each student can taste. Popcorn is always a winner. Something they don't usually eat is also inspiring.

**4.** Have students dictate to you (grades 3 and 4 can write their own) a story, in the first-person persona of the food itself, about how the food likes to be prepared, and how it likes to be eaten. Add lines about what it's made of, where it comes from, who makes it, and how it's used.

## SIMILE SMELLS

Grades: 1–5

Cross-curricula: Health

Preactivity Class Reading: "Smell!" by William Carlos Williams[4]

Bring some perfumes, oils, essences, flavorings, or particularly fragrant objects into the classroom in sealed plastic baggies.

**1.** At the beginning of the lesson, have students shut their eyes. Have their pencils and papers ready. Instruct them to write down immediately what the scent smells like. If they can't be specific with a simile, ask them to write any words that come to mind.

**2.** Make this into a short writing task detailing all the memories and associations connected with smells. Do they need to smell it again? Are there other words or things that it makes them think of? With each odor, have them write what it smells like.

**3.** Take another, more familiar smell or odor around the classroom, and ask students to remember where they first smelled it. Write some similes describing the smell. Rather than saying, "Vanilla smells *like* . . ." or "Vanilla is *like*," you might have them try a direct metaphor: "Vanilla, the first time at the amusement park . . ." Then ask them to connect it with the feeling or wish they had then: "Honeysuckle in the backyard/when I fell and no one was home./I wished I had wings. . . ." "Chocolate chips/I snatched spoonfuls/of cookie dough, scared I'd get caught. . . ."

## SYNESTHESIA POEMS

Grades: 1–6

Cross-curricula: English

*Synesthesia* is the phenomenon whereby one type of physiological stimulation evokes the sensation of another. I found several teachers who use this exercise for a creative writing jump starter.

Hearing a musical instrument can evoke images. Smells are notorious for evoking tastes, images, and memories. You might say that certain tastes feel like a smack in the face. It takes a poet to describe the endless possibilities of this scientific mixing of the senses.

Depending on the age of your students, you can start with a list on the board or just assign the writing and see what happens. If you discuss it first, take some suggestions from the class for each of the senses and write a group chain reaction poem. For example, what does the smell of fish sound like? What does the sound of the ocean crashing taste like? What does the taste of lemon look like? What does the sight of a fire feel like? What does the feeling of a slug taste like?

With older students, you can ask them to put the gerund form into the poem in every line. For example, "The sound of breaking glass, *shattering* in the kitchen, feels (tastes, smells, looks) like electricity *coursing* through my skin." But try to stick to the importance of the transference of feeling from one sense to another, and only add *ing* words if they illuminate that feeling.

Ask older students who grasp the concept well if they can create a triple synesthesia haiku: "At the sight of blood/I taste the sting of losing/a tooth to baseball."

*Spring Song (The West)*

as my eyes
look over the prairie
I feel the summer in the spring

—Ojibwa[5]

## CHANGE POEMS

Grades: 4–6

Another type of synesthesia poem comes from the cultural tradition of educating and entertaining through the spoken word. The Ojibwa song above is similar to many types of Native American oral poetry in that it mixes the senses.

Sometimes changes occur so slowly that we don't consciously notice them, but we feel them. They happen in our family, on our faces and in our hair, at school and work, in our hearts, and especially in weather and time. You can see the second hand move but you can't see the hour hand move. You can see that the sun is setting but you can't tell if it's moving. You know your hair is growing but you can't feel how fast.

Kenneth Koch suggests that to convey such feelings to us a poem "has to be a little shocking and surprising, as this one {the Ojibwa song] is in several ways." He suggests writing "a short poem about some surprising feeling you've had about time or change—feeling the past in the present, the spring in the winter, the day in the night, the night in the day, whatever."[6]

**1.** Brainstorm a list of the things in which students have noticed changes in their physical environment and appearance. Through what sense did you notice the change? What caused these changes? What can be done about time going by?

**2.** Write a group poem in which you answer the question of what one can see about the future by looking at the changes of the present. Use some of the changes from the list. Use yourself as an example and write a stanza for each of the five senses.

> As my nose catches
> smells from the train tracks
> I taste summer's first honey suckle
>
> As my eyes
> look into the mirrored sky
> scraper I feel old
> in the busy street of time
>
> —Aaren Yeatts Perry

**3.** In the fashion of the Ojibwa saying, ask students to write a draft of a poem in which they look at themselves in a mirror and try to notice something that is changing, slowly or suddenly. Tell them to write a stanza about themselves, rather than the outside world, for each of the five senses.

Ask what they have noticed lately when looking in the mirror. Have they had a peculiar feeling for the first time, or thought that they looked differently? What can they feel about the future when they look at their body?

> As my tongue tangles
> with the close up of metal braces
> I taste a beautiful smile in the distance.
>
> —Aaren Yeatts Perry

## HIDDEN ELEMENTS POEMS

Grades: 3–6

Any word that contains more than a few letters will contain other hidden words. *Electricity*, for example, contains the word *city*. But it also contains the letters of the following words: *letter, reel, elect, electric, lyric, icy*, and so on. ("This poem elects the letters of an electric, icy lyric to reel in critics.") The word *windstorm* contains the letters of these words: *words, drowns, worms, worst, sow, snow, stir, moist*, and others. ("Worms drown in a moist snowstorm, stirring like the dim words of the mind's wisdom.")

**1.** Make a list on the board or on a worksheet of some of the words from your recent science lessons. Try words like *dehydration, evaporation, cumulonimbus, hurricane,* the name of your state, *mealworms, aquarium, planetarium, terrarium, hippopotamus.* It may help to write the same word backwards as well so that students can see other letter combinations.

**2.** Ask each student for a word from within the key word. See who can come up with the most words from each one. With the list of words extracted from each spelling word, students should be able to write a found poem.

**3.** As with other found poems, the extracted words themselves will not be enough to use for writing very many complete sentences. Make it clear that students can use articles, pronouns, conjunctions, and similes. But suggest that they try to go outside the found list of words as little as possible at first.

Another approach to this kind of etymological research project is to take the words found with the vocabulary word and use them in a sestina, with the vocabulary word as a title. Sestina instructions are in the English chapter.

## ROCK

Grades: 3–6

Cross-curricula: Social Studies, English

This exercise is a good writing accompaniment to any unit on the early European settlers/Pilgrims, Native Americans, landforms, or dream stories. It can be assigned in anywhere from one to four phases, with a paragraph as an outcome goal for each phase.

**1.** Bring in some rocks, large or small, that look old. Place the rocks in view of the class. Explain that a long process was required to make the rocks and that they were here long before any people. Explain that the rocks contain history. They have ears and eyes that have experienced many things. They are, in a sense, our elders. Since the rocks can't necessarily say or tell stories, the poet's job is to listen to the rocks and learn the history. This may seem slow or make some students restless at first. But take this opportunity to explain the *muse* to the students—that it is an important task of any good writer (like scientists, artists, teachers) to muse upon things that are not apparent to others, and to record the results.

**2.** Have students come up to the rocks one at a time and listen to them. Spend as much time as possible listening, reiterating that the rocks do know things. Ask students to shut their eyes, open their minds, and hear what the rocks say about what it was like here in this land when it was inhabited only by American Indian people. The rocks may not speak in full sentences, but they can give phrases describing voices, food, work, landscapes, climate, weather, and interaction between tribes.

**3.** Write single words or phrases on the board. What Indians, what animals, weather, activities existed then? What relationship did the rock have with those people? Was the rock used as money, to build houses, for fire pits, dams, for telling the future, hunting, writing? Is the rock telling a story or just describing the environment? Is it speaking in an "I" voice or in a "we" voice? Individual or group poems in free verse can be written using these words.

**4.** Next, have each student hold a rock. Discuss the rock's weight, its hardness, its potential power. Have the rock tell them the dream it had when it first knew that the explorers were coming. How did it know in the dream? What changed in the weather, animals, surroundings? What sounds and sights appeared in the dream? Did the Native Americans of that place know that other people were coming? Could the rock tell them? Did the rock itself change in the dream? How did this make the rock feel when it woke up? The poem does not need to be called a dream poem or even mention the dream. The poem will be in the description and feelings ascribed to the rock.

*Many Hunters*

We used to guide creeks to the ocean.
We sang with the water in swishing clogirgleclick language.
It was so quiet you could hear rainbows bending over buffaloes.
The buffalo and the elk were our friends and we tried
to tell them to run and hide, that many hunters were coming.
But so many people were speaking in strange tongues
that no one could hear anything anymore.
The boat people came and hit us together
until we were forced to give them fire.
The boat people made houses out of us
but now we listened to their secrets at night
and now we're telling.

—Aaren Yeatts Perry

**5.** In the next section, write a poem in which the rock tells of what it witnessed when the explorers arrived. What did it witness going on among the Native American people, the explorers, and the slaves? How did the three different peoples use or treat the rock? What did each say to the rock? Did the rock speak to any of them?

Any of these poems may be written in present tense, as opposed to past-tense dream sequences. A final poem in the series can be written in which the rock explains how it feels now, looking back on this history. This exercise can support any study of Native American traditions. Also, a large conch shell can be used instead of a rock for the group activities. This activity was recommended by poet Lamont B. Steptoe.

*Mud*

Mud is telling me
not to jump into it
because it does not
want to be bothered.
But I really want to.
You will get dirty
if you jump in me.
Now shoo, and leave
me alone kid.
But I tried to
jump in anyway
and missed
and he said,
that is what
you get.
So he
left.

—Charles Welsh (Grade 4)

## CONVERSATION

Grades: 4–6

Cross-curricula: English

Preactivity Class Reading: Frank O'Hara's "A True Account of Talking to the Sun at Fire Island"[7] and William Blake's "Ah Sunflower"[8]

In the rock poem exercise, students draw on the wisdom of inanimate objects to tell them things about the past. In the conversation poem, the writer has a conversation with a natural or inanimate object that tells what it knows about the poet.

In William Blake's poem, the poet seems to know exactly what the flower is feeling. In Frank O'Hara's poem, the poet is awakened by the sun and has a whole conversation. The sun knows what the poet is going through, and offers stern but friendly advice.

**1.** Read O'Hara's poem to the class. Ask students what they noticed about the conversation between the poet and the sun.

**2.** Write a group poem with students suggesting lines in which the school building talks to the janitor at night. How does the building introduce itself? How does it know so much about the janitor? What has it noticed over time, and what does it suggest to the janitor? What are the janitor's responses?

**3.** Now have the students write their own conversations, preferably using an inanimate object at first: a sign, a hydrant, an alley, wall, tower, bridge, window, roof—something the student passes everyday. Apply the same scheme to this conversation.

**4.** Then go back to the natural elements. Now that there is an understanding and a trust in the process of conversation, the students can work with something living. Any natural element or weather form can be used. The same questions apply. Try to focus on a brief encounter between the natural element and the student. What is so important about the particular time the rain or river or fire or hail or wind began talking to this young writer? What did the natural element discover in the poem?

## I'M ZOO-LOGICAL

Grades: 2–5

Preactivity Class Reading: William Blake's "The Lamb" and "The Tiger"[9]

Countless poems are written about animals and the animal kingdom. Students can have fun pretending to be animals or exhibiting knowledge of the animals they choose to write about. The animal world is a traditional source of inspiration for the poet. It has typically been drawn upon as a passageway through which the artist enters and draws power, inspiration, and insight from the "spirit world."

Students can choose an animal and do an "I Used to Be/But Now I Am" poem, going into depth about what it was like when they were that animal, then explaining how they became what they are now. Will they go back to being that or another animal? Can they now have special relationships with animals?

**1.** For the early grades, try "bringing" an animal into the classroom. Go out into the hall, lead the (invisible) animal into the classroom, and tell students to be quiet so as not to scare it.

**2.** Find out what kind of animal it is by having students approach it one at a time, touch different parts, and pet the animal. Tell them to describe what it feels and smells like. They now have to name it.

**3.** Have them bend down to the mouth of the animal and listen to see if the animal will tell them anything. As in the conversation poems, students will find that the imaginary animal has quite a bit to say to them. This can be written in their own poems or in a group poem on the board. It should be very quiet for this section.

**4.** Then have students each bring in a very small animal and put it on their desks. Now students can write their own poems focusing on detailed physical descriptions of their animals, the moment when they found each other, how their animals got their names, any special powers their animals have, and what their animals tell them about themselves.

## PLANETS POEM

Grades: 2–6

Cross-curricula: Social Studies

Preactivity Class Reading: "Planetarium" by Adrienne Rich[10]

Planets are a great source of wonderment for us all. Students in the elementary grades enjoy discovering other worlds and exploring the concepts of space. Discoveries will continue to be made about our own galaxy.

Second- to fourth-grade students who are beginning to study the solar system can write haiku or renga describing what they know about each planet. The poems can be written from the perspective of someone standing on the planet or from what is seen through a telescope. When the poems are complete, students can draw a big orange sun in the middle of a paper. They can use hard-edged round objects of various sizes to trace circles indicating the orbit of each planet around the sun. On each of the orbit lines, students can now write their poems, spreading the words out evenly around the orbit.

After students are versed in planet names and their relationships with the earth, try having the students visit their favorite planet on an imaginary poetic voyage. On this research trip, have them be scientist-poets whose job it is to describe accurately and uniquely the elements as they are experienced on the chosen planet. Have them make as many comparisons as possible with earth. Have them make a discovery while visiting and include their findings in their poem. Would they like to stay or come back to earth? Does anything unusual or challenging happen to them while visiting? Who owns this planet, and is it O.K. to visit there and take things back to earth?

After students have a grasp of outer-space phenomena and the language of space, have them discover their own planet. How did they discover it? What and how did they name it? Who or what rules it? As gravity is to earth, what is the most powerful force on their planet? If they live there now, why is it better than earth? Is planet hopping allowed or are they stuck? Do they invite people over from other planets? If so, how do they play or work with them? What do they need to live?

In Adrienne Rich's poem about an unknown female astronomer, listed in the notes, she describes the shapes of the constellations. Try assigning this type of poem to your students for homework. Ask them to spend at least a half an hour staring at the constellations and to write down the shapes they see. Name them. When they bring them to class, ask them to write a ballad or story poem involving the characters or the named objects they saw.

*My Life Is Jupiter*

My hard life
is boring on earth
that is now.
That's why I moved
to Jupiter and moved
with my life and my friends.
And in Jupiter
none of the drugs
will come with me. . . .

—Gabrielle Mondesir (Grade 3)

## ARCHITECTURE

Grades: 3–6

Cross-curricula: Human Values, Social Studies

The scientific methods of observing, introducing new elements, and recording detailed descriptions of reactions can help enrich one's experience of architecture. In most cases, architecture is introduced into a human environment. This or that building or bridge either enriches human interaction or degrades it. For this writing exercise, it is the human being that is introduced into the architectural environment.

**1.** If you are conducting a unit on architecture, focusing on the Great Pyramids or the Great Wall of China, the prerailroad canals in your area, or Greek columns, then you will already have plenty of material. If not, you can have a discussion with the class and make a list of yours and their favorite and least favorite architectural experiences. In and around what structures do you feel the best/worst? What do they remind you of? Are they welcoming or foreboding?

**2.** Then make a list of as many different definable pieces of architecture that you know of: the door of a church, the rose window, the flying buttresses, gargoyles, vaulted domes, spires, windows, doors, stairways, porches, foyers, stoops, street lights, plazas, alleyways, columns, walls, parks, cobblestone walkways, fountains, bridges, atriums, skyscrapers.

**3.** Become one of the pieces of architecture that you enjoy the most. How do you feel maintaining that position for so long? What shape are you? Can you be compared to a letter, number, plant, animal? Does what you are made of make it easier? How long have you been there? What do you want human beings to notice that you are doing for them with light and sound and space and weather? Even if you are stationary, what is the motion evoked by your shape? Are you, as a piece of architecture, designed to help people or make things tough for them? Have you overheard or witnessed things that you would like to share? Or do you know secrets that you're not telling? What does your future look like, judging by the other architecture around you?

## THE DROP THAT WOULDN'T STOP POEM

Grades: 3–5

How many measurements of water can you fit in a poem story?

**1.** Start with a lonely drop of liquid who is looking for friends. What kind of liquid are you? With the class, make a list of liquids, long enough so that each student has a choice of one to begin with. Have students try to remember and list five different sets of friends they tried to play with.

**2.** These can be described using standard measurement if students need practice, or using invented measurements—bathtubs-full, hubcaps-full, cowboy hats–full, thimbles-full.

**3.** Did the droplet not like the way the liquid was moving (sloshed, splashed, globbed, sat still, rushed, flowed, etc.)? Was it too close to a solid? Did they mix liquids, starting off as egg yolks and ending up as Russian dressing? Was one group of liquids too opaque, translucent, transparent, or reflective for the droplet?

How did the droplet decide to move on? Where did it finally end up living? In mustard, honey, wine, fruit punch? In what container, doing what? How does it "behave" now when poured? How does it "interact" with its container? What about when new things are "introduced"? After finishing the story of the droplet, some students may have enough information to try another type of poem.

"I Used to Be . . ." poems are great when applied to weather. See how many stages in a row the students can include in their knowledge of weather transformations, beginning with a body of water, evaporation, condensation, a storm of some kind, drops of water, back to a small and then a large body of water.

## BUGS

Grades: 2–6

**1.** During a unit on insects, list on the board the names of all the insects you have studied and that students know about. Name a special characteristic or tendency that makes each one unique.

**2.** Ask the students to write a haiku or other very short poem about their favorite insect.

**3.** See if students can fit into the haiku their favorite thing about that bug. Is its name unusual? Does it have spectacular colors? Does it change forms? What does it do to protect itself?

These are always good poems to have illustrated and displayed. They may also be collected and displayed on one of the lanterns in the Arts section.

*A Bug*

A bug is nasty.
A bug could be friendly too.
It goes on a leaf.
A bug is ugly.
A bug could squirt a color.
A bug has a home.

—Omar Muñoz (Grade 3)

## CONSUMPTION POEMS

Grades: 4–6

Preactivity Class Reading: Ishmael Reed's "Beware: Do Not Read This Poem"[11] and Mark Strand's "Eating Poetry"[12]

In his usual form of deep satirical parable, Ismael Reed's poem eats the poet and the reader, like a newscaster reporting from the scene of some terrible quicksand. The Mark Strand poem has the writer eating an actual page of poetry in the library and going toward the librarian with equal hunger.

**1.** Ask your students to write a poem in which they eat the poems they have written. What do the poems taste like? What do they have to pick out that is inedible? How do they serve the poems, and how do they consume them? Are the poems fast food, home cooked, fresh off the vine, roots dug up from the ground, something hunted or fished?

**2.** Now reverse the assignment. Have the poems consume something. To have the poem consume the poet would be too close to the Reed poem. It can consume someone else. But if it does so, it must describe it in detail. How does it approach and hunt or prepare its meal? Can it be compared to any other hungry animal, or does it consume its victim slowly, like quicksand, water, fog, darkness? Students should use the poetic elements they have learned.

"Now the similes in this poem are creeping up on the school. The similes in this poem are now swallowing bricks like the desert gulps water. The alliterations in this poem are licking the lavatory lights and laughing. Listen, the verbs are crunching the caf with kids crying . . ."

**3.** Ask students to take the idea seriously and think about how various media consume time and energy. They can use scientific principles in the poem to create metaphors for consumption. Fire consumes air. Cold stops movement. Leaves consume sunlight to release energy, and consume water and carbon monoxide to produce oxygen.

Hand pad pen
Hand chalk board
Knife blade fruit
Fingers scissors papers
Battery livewire lightbulb
Magnet paper sticker
Books pages words
Mind work sweat

## ROCK, PAPER, SCISSORS

Grades: 3–6

When students are learning to describe systems of interacting objects, ask for a jumprope chant that lists interacting objects, similar to the old hand game of Rock, Paper, Scissors.

Trilogies of objects that work as a system don't have to beat each other. These should be systems that complete each other They should appear in the order in which they usually function. The secret to this exercise is to find sets of words that have the same number of syllables or rhyme internally. Quartets will create a different rhythm. Notice the difference in readability when plurals are used. With too many *s*'s, the lines are harder to pronounce and more sibilant. Some work well in the mouth and some do not.

Hammers drive nails.
Drivers nail screws.
Nails screw frames.
Screws frame canvas.
Frames canvases walls.
Canvases walls space.
Walls space people.

As with any poem, the more consistent its rhythm, thematic content, and form, the better it will be. These poems may or may not deserve an editing. They are fun to read back to the class, especially if the author achieves good syllabic meter and if the reader has a good presenting voice. Most important, they show the author's awareness of interactive systems.

A related exercise that is really a mind twister is to see how many words you can find that can be an object, a verb, and a subject. If these are concrete poems then they should probably be called "cement mixers." At first, try a chain reaction poem. Later, see if you want to develop it.

## NOTES

1. From publicity material for Richard Rhodes, *Dark Sun: The Making of the Hydrogen Bomb* (New York: Simon & Schuster, 1994).

2. Frank O'Hara, "Autobiographia Literaria," in A. Paulin, Jr., ed., *Contemporary American Poetry* (Boston: Houghton Mifflin, 1985), p. 375.

3. Carl Sandburg, "Numbers Man," and "Arithmetic" in *Harvest Poems 1910-1960* (New York: Harcourt, Brace and World, 1960), p. 59.

4. William Carlos Williams, "Smell!," in Robert Bly, James Hillman, and Michael Meade, eds., *The Rag and Bone Shop of the Heart* (New York: HarperCollins, 1992), p. 7.

5. Ojibwa, "Spring Song," in Michael Spring, ed., *Where We Live* (New York: Scholastic Magazines, 1977), p. 137.

6. Michael Spring, ed., *Where We Live* (New York: Scholastic Magazines, 1977), p. 214.

7. Frank O'Hara, "A True Account of Talking to the Sun at Fire Island," in Michael Spring, ed., *How We Live* (New York: Scholastic Magazines, 1977), p. 35.

8. William Blake, "Ah Sunflower," in J. Paul Hunter, ed., *The Norton Introduction to Poetry* (New York: W. W. Norton, 1985), p. 344.

9. William Blake, "The Lamb" and "The Tiger," in Alexander W. Allison et al., eds., *The Norton Anthology of Poetry, Revised* (New York: W. W. Norton, 1975), pp. 546–553.

10. Adrienne Rich, "Planetarium," in J. Paul Hunter, ed., *The Norton Introduction to Poetry* (New York: W. W. Norton, 1985), p. 234.

11. Ishmael Reed, "Beware: Do Not Read This Poem," in J. Paul Hunter, ed., *The Norton Introduction to Poetry* (New York: W. W. Norton, 1985), p. 433.

12. Mark Strand, "Eating Poetry," in A. Paulin, Jr., ed., *Contemporary American Poetry* (Boston: Houghton Mifflin, 1985), p. 532.

# 7

# Social Studies

This chapter contains poetry-writing exercises centered around some of the standard social studies content areas, such as a naming ritual; a social studies review Word Bag; debate and opinion; exploration of the perfect city; praise for cultural, political, and family heroes; magical powers; social relationships through self-control; and the cultural and personal relevance of clothing, social contrasts, professions.

These exercises provide short, enjoyable poetic field trips into the wide world of biography, citizen participation, speech and debate, historical documentary, and journalistic poetry. Later, when students are in high school English literature, economics, or history classes, they will have had the valuable experience of gaining a personal grasp of these issues.

## NAMES POEMS

Grades: 4–6

Preactivity Class Reading: *New Age Name Book*[1] and *6000 Names for Your Baby*[2]

During a social studies unit on famous figures who have made great historical contributions, you can conduct a poetry name study. Where did people like Denmark Veasy, Malcolm X, and Sitting Bull and places like Wounded Knee and Death Valley get their names? What do their names mean? Each student can pick a person or a place related to American history, research it, and explain the origin of the name. Some of them (Four Corners, New Mexico, or Yellowknife, Manitoba) lend themselves to poetry. Others will inspire prose.

During a lesson on the naming customs of other cultures, have each student explain what his or her name means. For younger students, this can supply words for an acrostic or diamante poem. For older students, ask them to write a free verse poem celebrating the meaning of their name, the form and style of which will better express their own personality and name.

In almost every preindustrial culture in the world, a ceremony is conducted around the naming of a newborn. In Native American sacred ceremonies, for example, a secret spirit name is given to an infant by senior members of the community. Other ceremonies are held to confer additional names when a child reaches adulthood. Most of these names are based on the personal character the child has developed. Adults who have watched the child develop base the name on his or her unique characteristics.

In Capoeira, for example, an Afro-Brazilian martial art dance developed by slaves in the sixteenth century and still carried on today, a baptism or *batizado* is held every year to name the new students. The master teacher "plays," fights, and dances with the young initiate and sweeps him off his feet without hurting him. The crowd of family and friends then yell nicknames at the new fighter that are characteristic of his unique features or ways. The master accepts one nickname and tells it to the youngster.

In poetry, members of your class can name one another on the basis of who they know themselves to be and who they want to be.

**1.** Use yourself as an example and write a list on the board of all the things you like and think are special about yourself. These should be qualities that make you the person you are.

**2.** Have students write as many lines as they can about what they think is special about themselves and what makes them the unique persons they are. Discuss the differences between qualities of personality and actions or deeds. Tell students to consult other lists they've made about themselves. If you have conducted some of the bodily awareness and self-esteem exercises, these lists will be in the poetry folders. Students should be able to produce a long list of things they like to do, things they like about themselves, and things they want to do or ways they want to be.

**3.** Do this exercise with students and read your list first. Tell them to write down any ideas that come to mind as they listen to you read the list. When you finish, ask if anyone has any suggestions. See if students can agree on a new and respectful name for you. For example, if you have studied the dragon form of kung fu and you also enjoy playing bridge, you might be Teacher Dragon Bridge during future poetry sessions. Be sure that students have a clear understanding of when it is appropriate to use these names.

**4.** Have each person read his or her list to the class. You may want to assign students the task of rewriting the list with "I am" before each item and an exclamation point at the end. Have each student read her list loudly and proudly. Listeners can write down names as they hear the list. Ask for hands of those who think they might have a good suggestion for a lasting personhood name.

## ONE POET'S GARBAGE

Grades: 3–6

**1.** On a photocopier, enlarge as many sheets as possible of words related to your social studies unit. Or bring in old magazines and newspapers with headlines on the same subjects. Letters that are at least one-quarter inch tall are more easily manipulated when being cut out.

Third-grade teachers, for example, may find headlines or articles on global geography and directions, skin color and racial identity, individuality and citizenship, community and local history. You can compile words related specifically to one unit of study or to a whole year, or collect words from two or more study areas.

**2.** Have students clear their desks except for a sheet of paper and a pencil. Explain what is going to happen—that you are going to go around and place a small pile of words on each person's desk. Make sure you don't put down so many words that students can't sort them out. Start with 10 or 15 each.

**3.** If you would like to create a group sample poem on the board, write one student's collection of words on the board. Have the student read the words to you one at a time. Write them randomly. Once the word list is complete, you can begin showing students the selection process that you would use. A bold word or phrase may jump out at you as a good title. Another strong word or phrase may make a good opening to the poem. Asking students for suggestions, you can build sentences and phrases with the rest of the words.

**4.** Have students turn over all of their pieces of paper so that they can clearly read each of their words. Have them choose a word they think will be a good beginning to a poem and place that word at the top of their desk. What word makes sense after that in a sentence? And what word would logically connect with that one? Encourage them to keep adding words together until a poem starts to come out. This is a good time to tell them not to sneeze or laugh at the poem so as not to blow the words away.

**5.** Circulate during this exercise to help students with questions and make suggestions. As soon as someone has something completed that they want to write down, collect the remaining words and allow students to write. They may come back for more words.

The difference between this approach and the general Word Bag in the English chapter is that the phrases and sentences constructed here by the students will be more likely to relate in content to issues they have studied.

Try including words from future lessons in the mixture as well. Sports headlines, advertisements, and social studies headlines make exciting Word Bag content.

## DEBATE POEMS

Grades: 5–6

Preactivity Class Reading: Dudley Randall's "Booker T. and W.E.B."[3]

Dudley Randall's famous poem "Booker T. and W.E.B." has the two famous African American intellectuals debating back and forth in grand poetic style.

**1.** Ask your students to choose two current or historical characters who opposed each other, about whom they have learned in social studies. Martin Luther King and Malcolm X, for example, disagreed on the issue of violence versus nonviolence. If there is a presidential or congressional debate this year, the two opposing sides can be set in a poem.

**2.** Ask students to present the two points of view in the poem in an "objective" fashion, leaving their opinions out of it.

*"The poet must also learn how to lead an attack."*
—Ho Chi Minh

## OPINION POEMS

Grades: 5–6

Now ask the students for their opinions on a variety of issues. Try to present them with some issues that have been resolved and some that are still in debate in the media. You may think you know the issues that your students think are controversial from discussion in the classroom. But when the topic is presented in this manner, they may come up with other topics you haven't heard them discuss.

**1.** Make sure there is a full range of issues on the board, and make sure students know that there are pro and con views for every issue. Encourage a full discussion of anything new and confusing for them. This can be a way for your students to broaden their vocabulary and speaking skills. But it is worthy of graceful precaution, as opinions will vary widely.

**2.** Have students help you write on the board the rough draft of one group "Fury" or "Together" (in the English section) poem reflecting opinions about an issue on which the whole class agrees. Edit the poem on the board. Then ask what some counteropinions might be.

**3.** Ask students to choose one of the issues from the Brainstorm list and write an address poem such as a "Fury" or "Together" poem. Tell them to begin by making their own mini-list of facts and feelings they know about that issue. Are there other details or clarifications that they need to include in their writing?

Remind them that if they include facts in the poem, the facts must be accurate. Have them choose another topic on which to write an opinion poem and assign it for homework so that their parents can help them.

## PERFECT CITY

Grades: 4–6

Preactivity Class Reading: Carl Sandburg's "Good Morning, America"[4]

There are good and bad things about every city. During a unit on urban life or civic law, you can make the following writing assignment. Can you conduct a role play in which you recreate city government with your classroom: city council, services, mayor, and so on?

Ask someone from the mayor's office to come to your classroom and give an overview of what it takes to run a city and what areas the city government is responsible for.

**1.** After reading the Carl Sandburg poem, discuss how your city compares to the one in the poem.

**2.** Make list of the things that are good and bad about your city. Make another list of the things you might see in a perfect city. Help students with the who, what, when, where, how, and why of business, law, parks and recreation, police, health, employment, education, arts, transportation, and other aspects of city life.

**3.** Ask your social studies students to write a poem that describes the perfect city. Rather than making this a "Not" poem, have them describe only what the perfect city "is" or "will be." They can write a "The Perfect City Is . . ." poem or an "If I Were Mayor . . ." poem. Elections? The poem can tell the story of a visit to the perfect city, during which the poet experiences all the accoutrements of such a city.

The "I Have a Dream" approach to this type of poem can be stretched through several lessons. Students can compose their own vision of the future in such a poem after studying local, state, national, or international problems. Encourage them to make it a solution-oriented poem by including lines such as "I see people driving in electric cars" or "I see kids going to schools where . . ."

## GLOBAL VILLAGE POEMS

Grades: 3–6

This is an effort to develop students' ability to describe and inform others of certain information. Poems like this one take the emphasis off the *I* in descriptions and strengthen students' awareness of the "other" as subject and object. This phenomenological approach also forces the writer's mind to capture what is poetic and fresh in a subject, instead of simply using preexisting proper names.

**1.** From your recent social studies units, list some of the most notable neighborhoods, cities, states, countries, continents, and planets in the galaxy. Discuss and list next to them some of the characteristics that make them not just well known but beautifully poetic. What made them independent, what battles were fought there, what groups formed them, around what ideas and beliefs?

**2.** Circle one place. Without naming it in the poem and without using the proper names by which it is known, ask students for words that help you describe the place (city, state, or country). Begin each line with the word *it*. California: "It lay there/on its squeaky bed/of gold-filled faults/big ocean in one arm/big desert in the other/snoring, quaking, snoring, quaking,/movie stars crawl like bugs on its legs/five hundred year old towering wooden goldy locks/around its head."

**3.** Assign students the task of picking one from the list and making as thorough a description as possible of that place. Make sure they refer to the place only as *it*. This will require them to include as many references to climate, weather, geography, culture, and population as possible.

## PRAISE POEMS

Grades: 4–8

Cross-curricula: English, Health

To write praise poems about anyone, the writer must have a strong feeling of respect or love for the subject. Anthologies are full of praise poems. Many praise poems are written by authors about other authors or artists.

**1.** Reread some paragraphs from a history book about the famous or not-so-famous historical figures you're studying in class. Make sure students hear about specific places, names, and events.

**2.** On the board, brainstorm a list of the person's notable, heroic, or unusual actions. As with the preceding exercise, list the special qualities that the person possessed that empowered the heroic action. How did the person get these qualities? Write a group poem to describe this character using *he* or *she* instead of *it*, as with the preceding exercise.

**3.** Have students write a short praise poem about the person in question, connecting the qualities with the actions. Focus on the human qualities: courage, patience, politeness, wit, strategy, strength, love. Include the emotions and feelings the person must have felt when transporting runaway slaves, running for president, saving lives, writing a famous book, and so on. What words will need to be used to reveal the identity to the reader without using the person's name? This exercise can also be done with famous authors.

**4.** The limerick form may also be used as a praise poem, since one of its most notable characteristics is as a commentary on a specific person. Although its intended purpose is one of witty humor, its concise rhyming form makes it a good, quick exercise for writing about someone in the positive.

In another writing assignment, students can write a praise rap poem using rhyming couplets for someone in their lives—a family member, someone at school, or someone else they know personally. Apply the same standards: The task of the poet is to convince the reader that the subject is worthy of great praise, without saying the subject's name. Watch out for the tendency to be too sentimental or too transparent. It's easy to write words like *nice, great,* or *wonderful*. Instead, draw out particulars like bodily characteristics. Do their hands, eyes, walk, or speech show anything about their lives? Do they have a special saying the poem could use as a base line?

Any nature-based lessons already studied by your students can be infused into such a poem. Use land or weather forms as similes and metaphors to invoke the qualities of their loved ones.

Acrostics, rap poems, haiku, free verse, and other types of poems can be used as forms for praise poems.

## MAGICAL POWERS

Grades: 4–6

Cross-curricula: English

Preactivity Class Reading: "On Being Extravagant," Henry David Thoreau[5]

This exercise is an opportunity for students to write an exaggerated, boasting praise poem about themselves. Here they can concentrate on the great qualities they have or wish to have.

**1.** Start by having them concentrate on a material object with which they feel powerful: a bike, horse, dog, car, house, ball, clothes, doll, guitar, shoes, or paintbrush. Starting with the material object can ground the thinking in reality.

**2.** Assign the writing of a poem that "lets loose" with the super-real or supernatural powers the object gives them. No modesty. Allow students to be as wild, big, spacious, flamboyant, and boasting as possible. Have them describe both feelings and actions. This can be a chant, list, parallel, or persona poem. It can be centered in a place, time, and event in which the power has full reign. The poem can be structured around an exchange (see conversation poems) in which the power object asks the poet to use it.

The power resides not in students owning the thing, but in who they are and in what they become when they are being the thing. If the poem starts to use television as a source of names, or cartoon power figures start to take over the poem, have the writers create their own names and qualities for their power figures. Have students use the present tense throughout the poem if possible.

When students read their poems aloud, experiment with ways of placing them in a physical position or context where the power can be felt, especially if they don't have a naturally theatrical or commanding voice.

## CLOTHING POEMS

Grades: 4–6

Cross-curricula: Science, English

Preactivity Class Reading: "You Were Wearing," by Kenneth Koch[6]

Clothing evokes the memory of its owner. Older students may want to interview their parents about an old piece of clothing that they no longer wear and rewrite the story of that garment as if it were theirs. The parent may be able to remember a deceased loved one through a piece of clothing. In these poetic tales, the clothing evokes time, lost or sustained: "She used to wear that cashmere scarf every time . . ." or "I let those chinos out so many times . . ." or "Ah, your grandfather in that hat and coat, looked like . . ." Even a single button contains a history of fingers and occasions. Another clothing memory poem by Conrad Aiken says, "These things do not remember you, beloved,/And yet your touch upon them will not pass."

Students can combine other subject areas and the clothing of other cultures for new poem content. They can use this language to explore how one thing "clothes" another. What is being hidden or adorned? What color garment, what style of apparel will evoke various moods, settings, and characters?

**1.** Have each student bring in an old article of clothing. Bring in a few from your own old clothes box in case some students don't have one. After they have put the article of clothing on their desks, propose to the class that someone else used to wear that piece of clothing.

**2.** Brainstorm a list of historical incidents, situations, battles, places, landscapes that you have recently discussed in a social studies class. List the famous historical figures associated with those places. Ask one student for a description of the article of clothing he has brought in. Put the historical character in that article of clothing and tell the story of how it was left behind and where the student found it. Write a group sample poem on the board in which a story is told around the article of clothing.

**3.** Ask the students each to write an exaggeration poem telling who wore the article of clothing and what event, problem, or fortunate incident happened to that person while wearing it that would have ended in its being left behind. What was left on it or in the pockets that tells a story about its former occupant or owner? Did a friend or anyone else notice it on the other person? How did the original owner finally discover who had been wearing the clothing? Try to use the names of the item's specific parts (cuff, collar, pocket, threads). Try one-word descriptions of its fabric and texture (scratchy, rough, silky, loose, tight) as if you were wearing it.

## IF THE SHOE FITS POEMS

Grades: 2–6

Cross curricula: Science, English

Preactivity Class Reading: "You Were Wearing," by Kenneth Koch[7]

**1.** Use time, weather, and land to begin this combination exercise. Make a list of 10 elements (rain, snow, wind, sun, night), then a list of 10 objects that one would find within the first object. For example, in the rain you find umbrellas, puddles, boots; in the wind, paper, kites, and trees; in the night, darkness, quiet parks, empty streets.

**2.** Now make a list of 10 articles of clothing. Write it vertically between the two previous lists. You should have 10 noun–verb–noun sentences, with articles of clothing acting as verbs. "Night coats frozen statues," "Wind boots kites," "Sun socks swimmers," "Snow sweatshirts hillsides," and so on.

When students start to get the hang and fun of this, have them add the words *in* or *with* to the lines you've written as a group, and complete them as poetic sentences.

**3.** Edit the rough draft or have students make their own list of 10 or 16 sets, if students want their sentences to be less nonsensical. If a student wants to write a series of lines using one natural element (night), 10 articles of clothing and 10 places within night can be combined to make a more thematically consistent poem.

## INSIDE–OUTSIDE POEMS

Grades: 4–8

One type of contrast poem is exemplified by Gary Snyder's "Mid-August at Sourdough Mountain Lookout."[8] This poem contrasts elements of nature almost as if they were photographic snapshots or film clips. The feeling of each line is brought out by its own seemingly accidental comparisons of hot and cold ("Outside white snow green pines/in here hot coffee and steam") or old and new ("A dandelion orange-green half open/the Rocky Mountains") or peace and war ("Black smoke from the cannon/young woman hangs up wash to dry").

**1.** Brainstorm a list of landscapes, homes, schools, buildings, and other living quarters occupied by historical figures from your recent social studies lesson. Add to the list contrasting opposites from a few local geographic locations with which students are familiar.

**2.** Ask students to give you a couple of lines for a group poem on the board that describes the opposites in the situations of warriors, explorers, discoverers, and various workers and professions.

**3.** The poems can contrast the sounds, sights, and feelings of the situations being described. They can include solids and liquids, stillness and motion, loud and quiet, living and dead, transparent and cloudy, or any external visual quality students can remember.

## CONTRAST

Grades: 5–6

In Walt Whitman's poem "When I Heard the Learn'd Astronomer,"[9] he contrasts a speech by the scholarly but boring astronomer with the simple beauty of the stars. The pleasure one gets from reading the poem comes from the contrast between the dry details of the lecture and looking at the sky itself. With words like *gliding, wander'd, mystical moist night air, perfect silence,* and so on, Whitman's description of the stars gives an easy, physical, and secret feeling.

**1.** First read the Whitman poem aloud and discuss it. Make a list of sample contrast options.

**2.** Then write a group poem on the board together with the class. This poem can be about listening to a lecture on healthful food and eating habits contrasted with the feeling and taste of actually eating a bowl of ice cream, a pizza, or a bag of chips; about studying the mechanics of a car engine contrasted with the feeling of actually riding in a car; or about hearing someone talk about basketball and how it feels to dribble, run, block, and shoot.

**3.** Have students write a poem contrasting something that is supposed to be important and something the student strongly feels is important. The students can then pick their own "serious" or "important" subjects and write their own poems. This is an opportunity for them to use curricular material. Some examples are to contrast the laborious study of numbers in math class with the way they use thousands of numbers at home every day; to contrast lessons at the library with the feeling, smell, sounds, and personal experience of a library; or to contrast a coach or referee telling the rules of a school sport with actually playing the sport. Or they can bring in personal examples.

It's O.K. to let students use simple satire. Making fun of something or mocking it is sometimes a good way to understand its seriousness. Whitman's poem doesn't tell the reader what to think or what the idea is. It simply says what happened in a certain situation and lets readers gather their own feelings and ideas.

## PROFESSION PERSONA

Grades: 3–6

Cross-curricula: Social Studies

Part of the anxiety of middle and high school comes from the unknown world of the workplace creeping up on some students. Profession poems give elementary students a chance to muse seriously about what it's like to work and what they want to do professionally. Many of the ideas and inclinations first expressed become their lifelong goals.

**1.** Have students interview someone in a profession that they are curious about. They should ask questions about job title, duties, favorite aspects, length of employment, pay, what and whom they see on a daily basis. You may want to have them bring this list back to class before the writing exercise.

**2.** One good way to write such a poem is to have students discuss the many different jobs and professions that they know about. Add to the list some of the most unusual professions that you know about in the fields of science, health, sports, entertainment, education, business, law, farming, and ocean science. Ask students to list the four professions they'd like to list first.

**3.** Then, choosing one profession, students should write out a draft of a group poem in which they pretend to have worked that job for years. They must describe with authority and conviction what they do every day, what they like and don't like, how they came to get that job, and what they want to do after it.

Someone might want to try to write a poem about the hardest job in the world, the most top secret, the most high paying, the most boring, the dirtiest, the funniest, the most famous, or the most glamorous or dangerous.

**4.** Now have students choose their own profession and write a poem from the perspective of a person who has worked that job or occupied that profession for years. Younger students can write a wish version, simply musing about what they could be.

*My Life (Excerpts)*

I want to be a scientist
and make a lot of money
to invent a lot of things
like a new flavor of honey.

I want to examine birds and stuff
but insects would do fine
to find out that their blood types
are not the same as mine.

I want to fix my city up
because it is a mess right now
but with the help of others
it could be turned around.

I want to have a family
of two kids and a wife
so when I die I could say
I lived a successful life.

—Leon Adside (Grade 5)

## I AM

Grades: 3–6

Students can "morph" into other personas very quickly if the other person is an athlete or music star. As you well know, whether from teaching or from your own children or childhood memories, nothing is as impressive or inspiring for the elementary student as the power of a famous person. Famous people appear to be loved, revered, and respected by the masses. And they appear to be welcoming, warm, and secure.

**1.** To develop further descriptive power in writing, students can become their favorite sports or music star. Ask them to list a few of the things that are so impressive about the personality on whom they are focused.

**2.** When students have a list and have read a few of the examples, ask them to write a present-tense poem in which they are that person in action. They should describe doing what the famous person does in as much specific detail as possible, with the immediacy of "I am performing now . . . ," not "When I am performing I . . ." Olympic stars can be recalled, as well as professional athletes and musical artists.

## CHANCE PLOT POEMS

Grades: 3–6

This plot-based writing assignment suggested by Palmer, Hafner, and Sharp,[10] starts with three sheets of paper. For this poetry-writing workshop, try a "deck" of 3"x 5" cards. They can be shuffled and returned more easily.

**1.** Give each student three cards. Write the following instructions on the board. Brainstorm a list of any of the lists if need be.

**2.** Ask that each student write the name of a place or setting from your current or recent social studies unit. Ask students to write the name of a famous person from any of this or last year's social studies lessons on the second card. On the third card have them write the name of a famous current sports, literary, or entertainment personality. To save time, you might prewrite one set out of three, then mix your cards into the deck created by students.

**3.** Collect the cards in three separate piles and shuffle them. Redistribute them to the class so that each student has one of each of the three sets. Each student should have a place; a social studies or historical personality; and a famous sports, literary, or entertainment personality.

**4.** With the plot characters, the students can simply write down a potential poem/story line. Now have students read these aloud to the class, one at a time. Peer observation of successful poem lines will give ideas to those students whose imagination is not sparked simply by the combination of characters.

**5.** If there is time, collect both of the personalities cards from each student, shuffle them, and redistribute them. Write down the new plots. Now ask students to write an outline for a short short story poem or a dialogue poem in which the fate of the two people is played out.

*Heroes Rap*

African Americans
We all want to hear.
African Americans
are always near.
Heroes with
Black power sincere.

Remember Barbara Jordan put the people in awes
She just wanted to make new laws.
She tried to make the people vote
So she could give the people hope.

—Statoya

Rosa Parks struggle is heard of a lot
She's the one that led the bus boycott.
She stood up for her right, put up a good fight.
She went to jail, but she got bail.

—Daliek

Langston Hughes
his poems couldn't lose.
Langston Hughes
He had a great pair of shoes.

—William M.

## HEROES RAP

Grades: 2–6

Because of the simple rhyme scheme, students of any age can create this type of rap poem. Hip hop and other forms of rap music, though usually in 4/4 time with the emphasis on the first beat, have far more complex lyrical schemes involved in their free-style poetry. This basic rhyming couplet scheme can be recited over a prerecorded blank rhythm track (with no lyrics), an electronic drum machine, a rhythm played on conga drum, or to children clapping.

**1.** Discuss some of your students' social studies heroes. List them on the board. Offer some suggestions as to famous figures in world history who have helped people and fought for scientific discovery, peace and justice, religious freedom, and so on. Talk about what makes a hero and why we need heroes, even if mythological. Abraham Lincoln is a good example of someone who heroically survived setbacks and went on to do other heroic deeds. Discuss the differences between people in what they hold in high esteem or consider exemplary behavior. Talk about community members, parents, and teachers as heroes.

**2.** Once you decide on a thematic area—Civil War heroes, Native American heroes, heroic scientists, heroes of Black history—have each student write a four-line rhyming couplet. Take turns reading and editing these as a group, especially if some are longer than average or too short.

As a group, write a chorus stanza about why we need heroes and what, in general, makes a person heroic. The class can memorize and recite this stanza together between the individual stanzas about classmates' chosen heroes.

An alternative individual assignment is an "I wish" poem in which each student focuses on his own hero and explores either what it would be like to be that person or what they would be doing if he or she were still alive.

## NOTES

1. Sue Browder, *New Age Name Book* (New York: Warner Paperback Library, 1974).

2. *6000 Names for Your Baby* (New York: Dell, 1983).

3. Dudley Randall, "Booker T. and W.E.B.," in Robert Ellmann and Richard O'Clair, eds., *The Norton Anthology of Modern Poetry* (New York: W. W. Norton, 1973), p. 869.

4. Carl Sandburg, "Good Morning, America," in Michael Spring, ed., *Where We Live* (New York: Scholastic Magazines, 1977), p. 39.

5. Henry David Thoreau, "On Being Extravagant," in Robert Bly, James Hillman, and Michael Meade, eds., *The Rag and Bone Shop of the Heart* (New York: HarperCollins, 1992), p. 163.

6. Kenneth Koch, "You Were Wearing," in Robert Ellmann and Richard O'Clair, eds., *The Norton Anthology of Modern Poetry* (New York: W. W. Norton, 1973), p. 1079.

7. Ibid.

8. Gary Snyder, "Mid-August at Sourdough Mountain Lookout," in Alexander W. Allison et al., eds., *The Norton Anthology of Poetry, Revised* (New York: W. W. Norton, 1975), p. 1272.

9. Walt Whitman, "When I Heard the Learn'd Astronomer," in Alexander W. Allison et al., eds., *The Norton Anthology of Poetry, Revised* (New York: W. W. Norton, 1975), p. 820.

10. Barbara C. Palmer, Mary L. Hafner, and Marilyn F. Sharp, *Developing Cultural Literacy through the Writing Process: Empowering All Learners* (Boston: Allyn and Bacon, 1994), p. 68.

# ▶ 8

# Human Values

This chapter provides poetry-writing exercises around the themes of self-esteem, cultural identity, family dynamics, and appropriate social behavior.

When a student is able to articulate feelings about himself, it can contribute to a sense of self-esteem and a good cultural identity. Teachers who encourage this can make their classroom a passageway to a place where students can be happy people. Poetry is a platform on which a student can proclaim his utter uniqueness in a way that sustains healthy social interaction and builds academic skills.

Some of these exercises encourage pomposity, strutting, and "voguing" as a way to experience high-end self-confidence for those who need it. Others suggest modes of introspection and honesty for those who need to step off the stage and simplify their act.

## I'M GOOD

Grades: 4–6

**1.** Start by having students write down a list of things they like about themselves in two different columns. This list of good qualities can be called positive power points. Use yourself as an example and have your students help you with the list of positive power points.

**2.** The first column should have qualities that the students are proud of and the second should contain actions or abilities they are proud of.

**3.** Then begin writing some rhyming couplets. The first line of each should contain a quality and the second an action to substantiate that quality. If they rhyme (*a-a* or *a-b-a-b*), it will create more intensity and make the couplets easier to memorize.

Begin with a simple opening line like, "I am great. I am good," and go from there: "I clean up the neighborhood./I am known for my good manners./I'll say a poem that makes you fly like banners." The poem can be boastful and declarative of the writer's fine values, qualities, and behavior.

Keep these lists of positive power points in students' portfolios and have them update their lists as you notice and point out improvements throughout the year.

## WE SO GREAT, WE

Grades: 3–6

Preactivity Class Reading: Gwendolyn Brooks, "We Real Cool"[1]

Try this poem when your students have all done well on a test or when they have just been on a field trip and information is fresh in their minds. This poem can be a vehicle for expressing that knowledge and excitement.

The classic "We Real Cool, Seven at the Golden Shovel" by Gwendolyn Brooks is about some students the author saw skipping school in Chicago. It is an easy poem to interpret and memorize for elementary-age students. The line breaks are crucial in setting the vocal tone and rhythm of the piece. She ends each line with the first word of the next line, but she pauses for the line break. Try reading the poem as it appears on the page. Have the students read it together while keeping time by snapping their fingers. The poem also contains excellent alliteration, internal rhyme, idiomatic phrases, and other surprises.

**1.** Discuss the predicament of the characters in the poem. The poem is observing the misbehavior of these truant students. Can your class turn this poem around and write a group poem in the same form, but one that celebrates their positive qualities as kids and brags about staying in school?

**2.** First try it on the board together. Have a discussion about the things that make them a good class. Together, list the qualities that make a good student. Depending on what is appropriate in your classroom, use their current slang for the word *good*. Besides *cool,* I have heard elementary students use the words *large, flip, fly, on, hip, excellent,* and *rad,* among others: "That movie was so fly."

**3.** Write a few of these simple couplets with the class before you assign individual writing. As with the Brooks poem, the lines don't have to make complete sentences. However, you should decide whether you will mimic the language of her poem or rely on standard English.

> We so great. We
> never late. We
> get good grades. We
> love parades. We . . .

**4.** Have students write a poem of their own, "signifying" about a list of things they are proud of.

*We So Cool (Excerpts)*

We so cool. We
stay in school. We
don't fight. We
are bright. We
get good grades. We
don't have AIDS. We
are smart. We
do art. We
don't fight. We
out of sight.

—Lydia Suarez (Grade 4)

## WORD SHIELD

Grades: 3–6

The saying that the pen is mightier than the sword is the basis for the following self-confidence poem. This is a writing exercise for creating a self-defense saying that students can repeat privately to themselves. In the conflict resolution section, there are several writing exercises that allow students to diffuse conflict with words. Here is an exercise that can work as a self-defense saying.

In a section called "Verbal Martial Arts," Canfield and Wells[2] conclude that discussing one's dissatisfaction, with the intent of improving conditions, is the most active and constructive method of responding to conflict.

**1.** First have your students review and add to their list of personal power points developed in the "I'm Good" exercise.

**2.** Younger students can start with the old expression, "Sticks and stones may break my bones, but words will never hurt me," and add some lines that match in rhyme or meter. The lines should include all of the student's own power points. "Sticks and stones may break my bones but words will never hurt me./You may choose to lie and curse but on my side I have honesty."

**3.** Older students can update and personalize the expression: "Drugs and guns may be your thing but you can count me out./Please don't bring that near my house or I'll do more than shout./I'll put your name in the paper, tell the neighbors too,/what I've seen you and your gang do."

**4.** A similar approach is a defiant "You Don't Know Me" poem. This is not meant to be said aloud but is a retort to be spoken to oneself. Each line should say something to the aggressor about what he is doing, acting like, or assuming and then rule it out with something better (from the power points list) about the poet. Make a good list of colloquial metaphors on the board as examples of aggressive threats that the poets can turn around:

> You might be tough as nails, but I'm hard as a hammer.
> You think you're bright as the sun
> but I can be cold as the night.
> You might think you know every trick in the book
> but I'm a library.
> You think you're bad with your slick sneakers
> but I can still walk away from you.

Yet another type of written verbal martial arts poem can be created using as inspiration Mbali Umoja's foreboding warning "Messing with a Poet Is a Dangerous Thing."

Once they are memorized, Word Shields can be carried around in one's chest (i.e., memorized) as a shield against verbal attack. Start by having students make a list of 10 persona metaphors ("I am a cyclone," "I am a steam roller"). Using forces of nature, weather, and the machine world, the writer can repeat a chant in which he or she becomes the object referred to: "I am a raging river, mess with me and you will be swept to the depths in great torrents of swirling water." "I am lava exploding in all directions. Mess with me and you will be burnt to an ember like a small town in my way . . . ."

> *Messing with a Poet Is a Dangerous Thing*
>
> When riled they've been known to cut throat
> with words.
> Once saw a poet take an insincere utterance
> and whip it to a frenzied chant that almost
> hung a man.
> When pushed into a corner, a poet will pull
> language rank and read you, I mean READ you,
> so you know you've been read to.
> Doing wrong to a poet take a brave soul,
> the risk being a poem with your name on it:
> actions recorded for all times.
> A poet got up on the wrong side
> can be the poet to avoid.

When you've just got to bug someone
and don't know who, grab a dancer or a painter.
But leave the lover of oral expression be.
The dialectic craftsman has a murdering tool:
the mouth of a poet provoked.
To send a galling jib might seem the funny thing to do.
But when you do it to a poet, beware.
The poet will answer you, maybe even in public too.
You see, messing with a poet is a dangerous thing to do.

—Mbali Umoja*

## I SEEM TO BE/BUT REALLY I AM POEMS

Grades: 2–6

Preactivity Class Reading: Gwendolyn Brooks' "The Ballad of Lincoln West,"[3] Frank O'Hara's "Why I Am Not a Painter,"[4] Carl Sandburg's "Four Preludes on Playthings of the Wind"[5]

"Not" poems are very popular with many teachers. They represent a simple but important compare-and-contrast exercise that is good training for descriptive abilities. Many noted and classic poems use this format. One approach is the group "Am/Am Not" poem.

**1.** First ask the class if there have been times when someone referred to them (or someone else) as something that they are not. Have them give you some examples and list these on the board.

**2.** If they aren't those things, then what are they? Now make a list of things they are. Have each student give you a unique example of something he or she is and is not.

**3.** Now create a freely flowing group poem with more examples. Afterwards, give the same assignment to student pairs and see what kind of contrasts are created.

*Crazy Circus*

I am courageous I am not frightened
I am black and pretty and special
  not yellow and blue
I am white not green, red not yellow

*Reprinted with permission of the author.

oh yes I am yellow
but a yellow orange sun
    burning, shining, warming, exciting. I am not
the cool moist earth sensible, grounded, serene.
    I am green but not mean
    I have been seen
    I am not cream
    a monkey NOT me!
I am purple not black
white not green
I am nice and gentle
a black lion
I am crazy I am not shy
pretty not ugly
a football player not a bird.

—Ms. Morris's group poem (Grade 3)
**Recommended by teacher and writer Catalina Rios**

Another type of "not poem" was suggested by Kenneth Koch, who uses Wallace Stevens's "Disillusionment of Ten o'Clock" as a model. Koch suggests that "one way Stevens makes his points in his poem is by saying what is not, and thinking of your poem as a 'Not Poem' might be a good way to proceed—that is, talk about something by saying what it's not . . . ."[6]

Ask your students to give a walking tour of their neighborhood using the same contrast approach to describe it or "antidescribe" it. Describe happenings and things that didn't happen, friends and people who are not, stores and shops that are not really shops, signs and elements of nature that "never were," memories of things that never happened. Sandburg's poem talks about a great city in a great nation, so great that "nothing like us ever was." Include feelings, night, day, things you never see, things you always see, places where the weirdest things happened.

Try the same exercise with specific lessons from your recent science or social studies unit. Remember, the writing is not saying that 2 plus 2 equals 5, or that clouds are made of potatoes, but that 2 plus 2 is *not* 5 and clouds are *not* made of potatoes.

The same thing can be done with the student's apartment or house. Give a tour—hiding places, rooms, furniture, toys, personal possessions, animals, food, pictures, beds, TV, play. Poetic elements include description, imagery, repetition, immediacy versus permanence, place.

As always, with a playful poem like this, it helps some students to work in a group. If you have a lot of children who live on one street, they may be able to write the poem together.

## BACK FROM THE FUTURE

Grades: 4–6

Cross-curricula: Social Studies

Writing down one's fantasies, goals, and dreams of the future is one way of testing them. By externalizing his vision, a young person can test and explore his options.

In the elementary grades, children can begin to imagine themselves in circumstances other than their own, including the future. One way to get them to write about this is by asking them to imagine being older and looking back on the time in which they now live.

Did they just turn 20, 30, 40, 90? Did they find something that reminded them of when they were in third or sixth grade? It's twenty years from now. Did they find a penny or a quarter with this year's date on it? A car from this year? A photo of themselves from grade school? Are they visiting their old neighborhood with their family? How have things changed? What have they done with their lives?

*Am I Alive?*

Back when I was a child I lived on Hancock Street.
It was pretty boring. I had hardly any friends at
all. We never went out because whenever anybody
went out they usually got shot at. That is why
when the children went out they acted like animals.
Every time the phone rang somebody else was shot
that I knew. Sometimes people we didn't even know
called to threaten the family. I was always scared.
I cried to sleep every night. The only time I was
happy was when I would come home from school and ask
my mom, "Am I alive?" And she would say yes. Now
I am 24 years old and it hurts me to see that
nothing has changed.

—Veronica Belpre (Grade 4)

*Back When I Was Ten*

My street was so boring.
My house was alright.
My family was good to me.
I felt lonely when I was 16.
I felt happy when I was 19.

Now that I'm 29 I feel great
because I now have a family
to take care of. The school
I send my children to has a
pool, dance class, aerobics class,
great teachers, and lots of other
stuff which I don't have.

—Christina Sierra (Grade 4)

## HAIKU BUSINESS CARD

Grades: 5–6

One of the key elements of good haiku is season. After studying various poetic forms, you may consider asking students to choose their favorite seasonal haiku from the year for a business card.

Students can draw lines with a ruler on an 8 ½″ × 11″ sheet of card stock paper to make as many business card–sized rectangles as possible on one side. In each rectangle, have them write the haiku of their choice. Of course, it will be easier if you copy one sheet of predrawn lines for the class. This way they can begin with the writing. Most copy centers will make multiple copies of card stock paper. Students must be able to write in very small letters.

When each one is filled, they can decorate and cut them out. On the other side of each one they can write their name and number and the word POET.

## I FOUND MYSELF

Grades: 4–6

Cross-curricula: English

Have students collect and cut out words from magazines and newspapers. This can be an arts-and-crafts exercise or a homework assignment. Some teachers have students bring in magazines over a period of time. Some go to a recycling bin to collect them or bring them in themselves in order to ensure some quality control in terms of content and direction of the cutouts. Tabloid publications with fantasy stories should be used in the English section workshop exercise called "Word Bag Poems" and may not work as well for this one.

This workshop seeks personal relevance and accuracy. Students should cut out as many words as possible and should understand the meaning of all the ones they use. The word search should include as many different sources as possible. Have students search for words that make them think of themselves. The words should include action phrases that represent things they would like to do, places they would like to go or have been, things they own or would like to own, people they admire, adjectives that fit them. Whole sentences should not be discouraged, but single words and phrases may be more dynamic. The more single words students have, the more creative they can be in constructing their found selves.

Have students carefully place the words on their desks and turn them over so that they are face up. Help them to begin arranging the words into phrases and perhaps sentences. A story or narrative poems with whole sentences may emerge. Then again, it may be choppy, whimsical. But all should be apropos to the student's identity.

As with the earlier Word Bag poems in the English section, some of the most complex verse can be created from what begins with a pile of scraps. This collection of cutout words can then be placed in an envelope or a bag, which can be kept and added to at a later time, thus giving students the process-oriented exercise of later throwing out words that no longer fit them or developing deeper descriptions with the ones that do. You may want to file these and pull them out later in the semester as a surprise.

## I REMEMBER YOU

Grades: 2–5

This is a game suggested by Canfield and Wells[7] that works well as a poetry-writing exercise. If the classroom is crowded, students can remain in their seats, but a circle is ideal for this word game. The premise is that students can invent and identify themselves with a poetry nickname created from the things they feel best about in the classroom, in their school work, or after-school activities.

**1.** Do a prewriting exercise in which you ask students to list three study areas (including sports, music, after-school activities, homework, etc.) that they feel they are good at, really like, or had fun doing. In what specific way are they good at the subject or activity? Have them name something special that they know about from studying that subject.

**2.** The warm-up round starts with the teacher. You begin by saying, "I am Ms. Masters." The first student follows by saying, "I am Veronique and that is Ms. Masters." Encourage students to pronounce their names like poets, "loudly and proudly."

**3.** For the next round, the rule is that each student says something that she is good at before her name. Have the students write down each person's statement before moving on to the next person.

**4.** Go around the class until the last person has recited this whole-group poem of name identifications. Make a compound word from the suggestion and add gerunds or participles: "I am book-reading Ms. Masters." "I am singing Veronique and that is book-reading Ms. Masters." "I am haiku Johnny and that is carol-singing Veronique and that is book-reading Ms. Masters." See how many names students can remember and repeat. It may be only three or four. Then start over as you continue around the circle.

An interesting version of this name poem exercise is to add a word before the name that describes how the student is feeling at the moment. "I am excited Ms. Masters." "I am shy Veronique and that is excited Ms. Masters." "I am proud Johnny and that is . . ."

After conducting the naming game, have everyone repeat his new name so that the whole class can hear it. Each student should write down the names and know who they are. Now ask the students to use the new names in a short poem in which they tell a story of something that happened with someone else or with a group of people in the class. They can tell of something they saw others in the class doing, with which they were not involved. Or they can use the names in a short poem like a limerick.

## FAMILY LOVE POEMS

Grades: 1–6

Reading: Edna St. Vincent Millay's "Love Is Not All: It Is Not Meat nor Drink"[8] and e. e. cummings's "somewhere i have never travelled gladly beyond"[9]

Have students consider what they've learned in science lessons about animals. How do animals show affection? What do monkeys and lions do to show care and affection to their young?

**1.** On the board, make a list of the things human families do when they want to show love: kiss, hug, joke, hold hands, wink, rub noses, walk together, give gifts, help one another do things, write poems, cross oceans!

**2.** How do other objects love one another? Ask the students for five imaginary examples of inanimate objects showing love for one another. For example, coffee loves milk. Lemon loves tea (see "Give Me Beauty" poems in the Art chapter).

**3.** Once students have a good list of their own examples written down, ask them to write a comparison love poem using the examples. Instead of *like* or *as* they can use either *the way* or *as long as* . . . : "I love you the way coffee loves milk to swirl around inside it until they become one." "I will love you as long as giraffes rub their long necks together like spotted desert lighthouses."

In the poems for family loved ones, try writing a poem in which the poet becomes the object of the praiseworthy person's desire. In e. e. cummings's poem "somewhere i have never travelled gladly beyond," the poet talks about himself as if he were a flower. The person he loves makes the flower blossom. What beautiful object does the person the student loves make him or her feel like? How does that object realize the student's love, respect, or inspiration?

Another approach is to try having students list the things they love about a given person. "The way you eat, sleep, talk, walk, look, wear your hair/clothes, play, work, study, swim, ride, blink, breathe, drink, etc., is like/reminds me of the way the wind loves the leaves by the lake . . . ." The more individual or personalized the thing the poet likes, the more poetic the comparative description will be. Keep the poems focused on pets, siblings, parents, or grandparents.

## MYTH POWER POEMS

Grades: 4–6

Preactivity Class Reading: "Amergin and Cessair"[10]

Read and discuss the short myth story listed above. If you don't have this book, have your students take turns reading a myth or legend of your choice. What elements make it a myth or legend? What did it explain that happened to the characters involved? Does it have to be true to be believable? What was the magical thing that someone was able to do or that happened in the story? Can students write a short poem saying what magical powers they have using language that is as exaggerated as possible?

Because of the magical and lyrical language of the myth poem, my students were inspired to write some of their own magical abilities poems. I gave them several different sets of opening lines—"I am . . ." and "My life is . . ." This class had great imagination and composition ability but just needed starting help.

*What Am I*

I am the fish that my father catches in Lake Erie.
I am the prince of the castle of snow.
I am a boy that is an owner of blue sky.
I am many little asteroids going through space.
I am the medium person in the family of life.
My life is a blossom that blooms in the light.

—Joshua Ferra (Grade 4)

*What Am I (Excerpt)*

My life is a bowl full of gummy bears.
It is full of cans to recycle.
When my life is standing up it feels
like water running down pipes.
If you turn my life upside down
it feels like an American hoagie.

—Daysi Roque (Grade 4)

## HALL SPY

Grades: 3–6

"Hall spy" poems are fun listening exercises in which students are asked to go into the hallway and write down the sounds they hear. This is a kind of audio journalism whereby students report in poetry on the sound stories they witness. McKim and Steinbergh suggest that the students go in groups.[11] Groups are fine if you're assigning hall spy poems to the whole class. This varies from school to school. I send a few students at a time and work with the rest of the class on another poetry assignment. On their own, students can concentrate on the sounds and tend not to talk. Send one student each to the first floor, basement, front entrance, cafeteria, and so on, to see what kind of variety they bring back. With students who come back with simple lists of sounds and who don't get much comparative writing, you might ask them to rewrite, including an added line for every sound that says what they hear "in" the sound or what secrets the sound "is telling me." If the student wrote only "radiator pipes," for example, you can encourage him to take it further: "In the radiator pipes' clanking I hear the heat of summer." (See the "Changes" poem in the Science chapter.)

I have also used this assignment when working in a classroom where the teacher sends a student to the hall as punishment. In one case, I was working with a class on African praise poems in which the West African word *ariku* is used to invoke the memory of one who has passed away. A child was sent to the hall, and I assigned a hall spy poem that he was to complete by the end of the class.

*Ariku in the Halls (Excerpt)*

In the doorway I stand at it is quiet
But now a boy running out of the classroom
With his loud footsteps.

It's like a jungle out here.
What a place to be.
This is the word I have for all the
silent classes:

ARIKU!
Kids throwing money in the air,
Boys cursing and ready to fight.
This is for the silent class:

ARIKU!

Kids learning
And for the ones who pay attention.

—Schuyler Durley (Grade 4)

## CROWDED OR EMPTY

Grades: 1–6

Some students have no one but the television to go home to. Others would love to be home alone with the TV sometimes because they are crammed into a house with too many family members. This is a lively self-concept topic for students to document each year.

**1.** Take a vote to see whether more students feel that their house is cramped and crowded or spacious and empty.

**2.** Ask students to write three columns of words describing what their house is like when they go home from school, what it's like at night, and what it's like in the morning.

**3.** Now write these pieces into a paragraph form or a parallel poem with a repeating line: "When I'm alone . . ." or "In my house . . ." Make sure students describe how they feel about how many people are there. Do they like it or not? Did anything scary or funny happen? Do they have any advice to others? How would they rather be? Would they like to address the poem to their parents?

These "Home Alone" poems are good scary poems for Halloween. Another similar exploration can be made into specific places that students find cramped or too empty: hospitals, grandparents' houses, stores, elevators, restaurants, classrooms! All of these have stories attached to them.

*What Is Being Alone?*

What is being alone?
Is being alone staying in a house by yourself
Or is it just a feeling you get when you're sad?
Is being alone sitting in a room by yourself
Or is it being in a room with people and not making contact?
Is being alone the fact that you are selfish
and don't want to be with anybody?
Or is it thinking no one cares about you?

—Kamila Whiters (Grade 3)

*The House Is Too Small*

I can't live here.
There is no air.
I can't even touch my hair.
This house is too small.
Can't you hear me at all?
This house is too small.
I feel like I'll fall.

I am in the kitchen.
There's no Gotdurn chicken.
I go to the bedroom
trying to lay down,
Bam! I fall on the floor.
My Mom, Dad, Sister, Brother,
Grandmother, Grandfather and more.

They all wake up saying,
Shut up that noise!
I told you this house is too small.

—Aisha McMullin (Grade 3)

## NEIGHBORHOOD MYTH POEMS

Grades: 4–6

Teaching poets such as Craig Czury recommend that kids do folkloric story gathering as a rich source for poetry. Many residents in your area will have migrated there from other parts of the United States or from other countries. The stories of the older people in the areas where you live partly define its culture. They have history and detail and music, all the laments of poetry, in their stories.

**1.** First, write the meanings of *myth* and *legend* on the board and have a discussion about them.

**2.** See if you can come up with a couple of examples of things for which there is no explanation and about which students have a deep and common feeling and could write a myth. If not, offer a few examples of things of which they do not know the origin, and about which they could create a myth: "How the Sky Was Invented," "Where Smoke Came From," "Where the Chill Came From."

**3.** A source of myth for which there is no match in terms of humor, science content, unusual story structure, wisdom, and brevity are coyote tales. As with any legend, like "Amergin and Cessair," students will immediately adopt and replicate the language and form of most stories they are told. See what kind of myths they are able to write before reading these, and make additional assignments afterwards.

**4.** Have a short storytelling session in which you ask your class if any one can relate a legend or myth from his neighborhood or family. If none is on the tip of their collective tongue, assign a homework task of interviewing their parents or grandparents. Encourage students to (1) get as much depth in one story as possible, (2) make sure it is based in a place, and (3) try to get the adult to refer to as many names and colloquial or idiomatic phrases (local expressions) as possible.

## ANCESTOR LEGENDS

Grades: 3–6

In *The Folk Lore Writings of Zora Neale Hurston*[12] she tells of the well-known southern folktale characters of "Daddy Mention," "Uncle Monday," "Mother Catherine," and the ubiquitous "High John De Conquer." Can your students create a legend using their own family members?

**1.** A good exercise to begin this is just to have the class write a couple of paragraphs about one parent, listing or telling about their relationship with the parent—what they do together at different times of the day, favorite memories, what the parent is known for.

**2.** If students have done family praise poems or love poems, they can use the list of things they like about a person to refresh their thoughts of them.

Ask them to add to the list any actions or deeds by the family member that seemed powerful or heroic, that saved the day or someone's life, or that seemed supernatural. The poem can be about a mysterious or kindly thing that one of their parents did and became famous for.

**3.** Have students choose one of the dramatic or eventful stories and tell about it as if it happened long, long ago. Begin poems with lines like "Long, long ago, when I was just . . ." or even "Once upon a time . . ." Traditional ballad openings will stir up the storytelling mode of writing.

Have students write a narrative or free-verse poem addressing their grandchildren. Ask them to imagine being 65 years old and telling their grandchildren this story. This way they can be as extravagant as they want, and they will include details for an audience that doesn't know the person they're talking about.

**4.** Have a fifty-years-later reading in which each student reads his or her poem as if fifty years had gone by since it was written. The simplest incidents always seem dramatic or important when told to family members fifty years later, especially when they are told at family gatherings over and over! This is how legends are made.

## PEN PAL

Grades: 1–6

Preactivity Class Reading: Kabir's "To Be a Slave of Intensity"[13]

It is excellent writing practice to correspond with a pen pal at a local college or university. The curiosity and learning potential between adult students from other places and your elementary students runs both ways.

Any poetry writing exercise can be a pen pal poem. One that drew some intriguing responses from my students was the neighborhood poem. I told them they could write "lie" poems or photograph poems, but they had to give a convincing picture of what a visitor would see who came to the child's neighborhood. Some became embarrassed, some proud and excited. The writings ranged from haiku to personal letters.

*My Street (Haiku)*

I have a block so
cool it has a court and swing.
You can come around.

—Joshua Ferry (Grade 3)

Dear Seth,
If you come to my house
you'll see yellow cars,
beautiful houses and hamburgers
falling down. I see
lions and tigers down
the corner store. There's a junk
yard in my store.

—Heriberto Velez (Grade 3)

The same type of poem can be done about the school. Ask the students to give a guided tour of the route they walk or ride to school. When they are finished, they should have a verbal picture book of their daily path. See if they can write it as if they were walking down the street. Give them some well-known tourism lines such as, "And this is the famous . . . ," "Now on our left we see . . . ," "This is where I once saw . . . ," and "My favorite part of the walk . . ."

If you do exchange letters with other students of any age, try sending a personal letter along with the poems. Ask your students to explain to their pen pals why they write poems, who their favorite poets are, what they like to write about, what their favorite type of poem is, and how they write poems. Any one of these can constitute a short writing assignment.

## MAGIC WORDS

Grades: 3–6

Cross-curricula: Social Studies

Preactivity Class Reading: "Magic Words" (Eskimo)[14]

First read the preceding selection together. You may want to start by reading it to the class yourself in order to invoke the seriousness of the issue. The poem talks about the abilities of people long ago to become animals and vice versa. It says that all beings spoke the same language and that the language was full of magic words that simply needed to be spoken in order to make things happen.

After the class grasps this concept, ask the students if they had magic words what the words would be and what they would do with them. From the discussion you may get some good ideas on which to improvise. If not, try a group poem in which the class invents a magic word to invoke or receive something.

Here's one for a straight "A" report card. You can explain to the class that, of course, the magic invocation won't work until the sayer has it memorized and believes hard enough in what she's saying (and studies harder!).

Hoodoo axe own
ipso saxophone
backbend backbone
data on telephone
human cyclone
straight a loan
umagammagroan
hoodoo axe own
ipso saxophone
straight a loan
umagammagroan

Another short writing exercise can be done by asking the students to imagine "a time when words were helpful."

**1.** Make a list on the board of good things that one person can say to another to be helpful.

**2.** Ask the children to invent onomatopoeia words that invoke what the kind words on the board mean.

**3.** Ask that they write a short poem story about a specific incident in which these words helped. What were the consequences in the community when people accidentally said these magic words?

Try the reverse of this and ask that they imagine a time in the future when people say nothing but good things to each other. Have them look back from the future and write a poem about a time when words were hurtful. What pain did the words cause? How? What were the words? Have things changed?*

*Recommended by folklorist and poet Beth Phillips Brown.

## ETHNICITY

Grades: 3–6

Cross-curricula: Social Studies

Preactivity Class Reading: "Coca Cola and Coco Frio" by Martin Espada,[15] Growing Up Italian" by Maria Mazziotti Gillan,[16] and "Funk Lore" by Amiri Baraka[17]

Ask the students how many know their ethnicity and ethnic ancestry. Have them take turns showing their family's country of origin on the world map and saying what they know about their cultural traditions. Do they know how to speak any words in their ethnic language? Any special foods? It is always helpful for students to know the story of their parents' and ancestors' lives.

**1.** Write some interview questions on the board that the students can copy. Have the students interview their grandparents in writing or on tape about special aspects of their lives. Ask them to get their parents to help write down the answers. Be very specific in the questions about the names, occupations, games, food, work, language (bring words), clothes, marriage, children, animals, dreams, crafts, land, travels of ancestors, incidents, successes, accidents, myths, hearsay.

**2.** Have students discuss and clarify their backgrounds, origins, and cultural heritage with their parents. Trace one particular relative as far back as possible. Some classes will include very recent immigrants and others will be composed of children of families who have been on this continent so long that they can only guess at their cultural ancestry.

**3.** Some students will come back with cassettes full of information. At any rate, you should be able to write a beginning ancestry poem. Assign a poem in which students remember the clothing, housing, work, food, and hobby of one particular relative or ancestor.

Other options include a list poem about what is "In My Blood"; a thank-you poem thanking ancestors (or a specific one) for the traditions the students still carry on; or a glorified "I Have the Powers of My Ancestors" poem in the form of the Celtic poem "Amergin and Cessair" listed previously. In this case, the ancestor can come to visit to tell the poet of his or her special names and powerful abilities.

**4.** If your class has a more homogeneous makeup, you could have students read children's poems from around the world. Have an international poetry reading in which you celebrate the great ethnic diversity in a multicultural society made up of people from African, Arab, Caribbean, Chinese,

Italian, Jewish, Mexican, and many other backgrounds (see the Bibliography).

## NOTES

1. Gwendolyn Brooks, "We Real Cool" in Alexander W. Allison, et al., eds., *The Norton Anthology of Poetry, Revised* (New York: W. W. Norton, 1975), p. 1169.
2. Jack Canfield and Harold Clive C. Wells, *100 Ways to Enhance Self-Concept in the Classroom* (Boston: Allyn and Bacon, 1994), p. 93.
3. Gwendolyn Brooks, "The Ballad of Lincoln West," in *Blacks* (Chicago: Third World Press, 1987), p. 482.
4. Frank O'Hara, "Why I Am Not a Painter," in Robert Ellmann and Richard O'Clair, eds., *The Norton Anthology of Modern Poetry* (New York: W. W. Norton, 1973), p. 1139.
5. Carl Sandburg, "Four Preludes on Playthings of the Wind," in *Harvest Poems 1910–1960* (New York: Harcourt, Brace and World, 1960), p. 59.
6. Kenneth Koch, quoted in Michael Spring, ed., *How We Live* (New York: Scholastic Magazine, 1977), p. 215.
7. Canfield and Wells, *100 Ways to Enhance Self-Concept in the Classroom*, p. 68.
8. Edna St. Vincent Millay, "Love Is Not All: It Is Not Meat nor Drink," in Richard Ellmann and Robert O'Clair, eds., *The Norton Anthology of Modern Poetry* (New York: W. W. Norton, 1973), p. 494.
9. e. e. cummings, "somewhere i have never travelled gladly beyond," in Alexander W. Allison et al., eds., *The Norton Anthology of Poetry, Revised* (New York: W. W. Norton, 1975), p. 1072.
10. Michael Meade and Erica Helm Meade, "Amergin and Cessair: A Battle of Poetic Incantation," in Robert Bly, James Hillman, and Michael Meade, eds., *The Rag and Bone Shop of the Heart* (New York: HarperCollins, 1992), p. 171.
11. Elizabeth McKim and Judith Steinbergh, *Beyond Words: Writing Poetry with Children* (Green Harbor, MA: Wampeter Press, 1983).
12. Zora Neale Hurston, *The Sanctified Church* (Berkeley, CA: Turtle Island, 1981).
13. Kabir, "To Be a Slave of Intensity," in Robert Bly, James Hillman, and Michael Meade, eds., *The Rag and Bone Shop of the Heart* (New York: HarperCollins 1992).
14. Eskimo, "Magic Words," in Robert Bly, James Hillman, and Michael Meade, eds., *The Rag and Bone Shop of the Heart* (New York: HarperCollins, 1992).

15. Martin Espada, "Coca Cola and Coco Frio," in Maria Mazziotti Gillan and Jennifer Gillan, eds., *Unsettling America: An Anthology of Contemporary Multi-Cultural Poetry* (New York: Penguin Books, 1994), p. 124.

16. Maria Mazziotti Gillan, "Growing Up Italian," in Maria Mazziotti Gillan and Jennifer Gillan, eds., *Unsettling America: An Anthology of Contemporary Multi-Cultural Poetry* (New York: Penguin Books, 1994), p. 382.

17. Imamu Amiri Baraka, "Funk Lore," in Maria Mazziotti Gillan and Jennifer Gillan, eds., *Unsettling America: An Anthology of Contemporary Multi-Cultural Poetry* (New York: Penguin Books, 1994), p. 156.

# ▶ 9

# Citizenship

This chapter includes conflict resolution games and poetry-writing exercises that build on social diversity. They are designed to help students work and play with the language of problem solving, mutual respect, and social ethics in a way that only poetry can.

Students who learn a variety of social and academic problem-solving skills will be better equipped to meet academic performance standards and make contributions to their community. Says former UNESCO Director-General Dow, "It therefore seems essential to identify, in educational systems, the factors that pander to selfishness, contempt for others and a taste for violence, along with the factors that encourage respect for others, develop a moral sense and inspire a feeling of brotherhood."[1] Poetry and other forms of creative writing demand such creative and transcendent responses to experiences of difficulty.

> *"The art of poetry is to touch the passions, and its duty to lead them on the side of virtue."*—Cowper

## WEB POEMS

Grades: 3–6

In any study of conflict, it helps to identify where and when problems begin and how they cause a chain reaction of further problems in groups.

**1.** In this exercise, bring up the idea of conflict and discuss its meaning. Ask the class for examples of conflict. When, where, and about what have they recently seen a conflict in their lives? Could a recent incident at school be classified or described as conflict? How about at home, on the street, or in the news? Remind them that the class is "about the result, not who's at fault." To illustrate this list of various cases and causes, conflict resolution specialist William Kreidler suggests drawing a "conflict web" on the board.

"In the center, write the word CONFLICT and circle it. For each example of conflict given by a student, draw a solid line from the main circle and add the word or phrase . . ." The web should look like a wheel of spokes. At the end of each spoke is a "trouble bubble" full of the suggested words: *money, work, school, family, ownership, cars, TV shows, food, violence, quality family time, drugs, noise at night*. "As students begin suggesting ideas related to those previously suggested," continues Kreidler, "link them not to the main circle but to the appropriate previous contribution."[2] This creates a visual web that shows how one conflict sometimes causes or leads to another. In discussing this, ask students to describe the results of each stage of conflict. Who was affected? What did it look and sound like? Did it lead to more trouble or did something happen to lead to a resolution, answer, safety, relief?

**2.** Make sure students copy down this conflict web and save it in their portfolios. Once the web is substantial enough to move on, ask a student to come up to the board and, using the web, explain how a conflict starts with a certain incident and where it goes from there. Have several students talk through the web lines of conflict. Try to ask students to tell you what each of these has in common with the others. What worsens each? And, as Kreidler puts it, "What cools it off?"

Are there special words to describe the feeling or situation when things are messed up, in-conflict, or problematic between the people in their lives? How do students feel when there is danger, confusion, or a problem? List some of these words on the board so that students can use them to describe their situation of conflict.

**3.** Have students prewrite their own examples of conflict. Make them as personal as possible. See if each student can come up with 5 to 10 examples. If they are stuck, they can title a stanza or paragraph "Conflict is when . . ." and begin every subsequent line with "and then . . ." followed by a description of the resulting chain of events. They can use examples from the board or others that they know well. Have them give details of the situations of conflict, including the words used, emotions, actions, and conclusion. Each line can be as long as it takes to explain the details of the conflict and its effects.

**4.** Now have a short discussion about peace (or resolution) as it relates to these conflicts. Which came first, conflict or peace? What might have caused the first conflict between people? Is conflict ever caused when someone wants to be happy but someone else is keeping them unhappy? What was the longest period of time during which there was no fighting and peace reigned throughout the world? How can peace be maintained? If conflicts like those listed here break out, how can peace, calm, happiness, a norm be recovered? Come up with some other words for *peace*.

**5.** Now add a peace line to each of the conflict lines. Begin with lines like "Peace would be when . . ." or "The way to peace from here is . . ." Ask students to end the peace line with a single word describing the feeling of peace.

Conflict is when
my parents send
me and my brothers and sister
to our room for playing
when our chores weren't done
but I had done mine.
Peace is when my brother and sister
admit it and tell my parents
to let me be. I'm free
to play all day!

## TROUBLE TRAIN POEMS

Grades: 4–6

**1.** Start the poetry exercise by drawing the engine and a few empty box cars of a "trouble train" on the board. Using one of the lines of conflict from the previous web, write the name of a conflict followed by a colon in the engine car of the train. The train will contain the words representing the chain of events causing problems. This is so students learn to "see the train coming."

**2.** Ask students for information about the conflict for every car that follows. If the conflict word is *fight*, ask them where, who, over what, why, what happened. Fill the cars with names of the people it affected and the chain of events as it moved down the line. How did it end? It is from this line of information that they will write.

**3.** After writing these inside the train cars, ask how this could have happened without a fight. The alternative ending suggested by the students can be placed in the caboose—for example, *fight*: school/doorway/who's first/who's best/scraped knees/torn up homework/principal's office—*patience*.

**4.** Ask the writers to choose one of the conflicts that you have listed on the board or on a worksheet and compose short, concise sentences in which the last word of each sentence is the first word of the next. This train-car repetition approach holds the poem together, reflecting the urgency and interconnectedness of the moments of the conflict.

A bad fight broke out at school
At school two bad boys hot for the door
The door to the yard shut tight waiting
Waiting to be burst by two out of line
Line broken bound to bet who's best
Best at hitting the fence first and last
Last one trips loser to skin his knee
Knee boy rolled into traffic
Traffic skidding like skin off bone
Bones of bad boy shaking in office later
Later with a big bloody lip
Lip of losers wouldn't be broken open if . . .
If he'd opened his mind and stayed behind.

The caboose line says what would have happened if the boy hadn't tripped the runner. Try to get the writers to create constructive endings with appealing alternatives to conflict.

Once students have identified the opposite of conflicts, you may want to assign a diamante poem. The conflict noun (one word) is the first line, and the peace noun (one word) is the last line. The second line (two words) contains adjectives that describe the first word. The third line (three words) has three participles about the subject in the first line. The fourth line contains four nouns that the first and last words have in common. The fifth line again has three participles about the subject in the last line. The sixth line has two adjectives describing the last word. And the last line is one peace noun, as described.

## COMMUNITY POEMS

Grades: 3–6

Have a short discussion about the importance of community and what makes up a community. Ask for examples of a community. This is a "teachable moment" for language in that you might take a moment to ask the class where the word *community* came from. Show the class the Latin, French, and Middle Eastern roots of this word meaning "common," "living together," or "fellowship." Discuss the difference between an individual and a community problem.

**1.** Ask students to tell you about a conflict in their community, neighborhood, town. On the board, list some of the causes, consequences, commonalities and differences between these conflicts. Make a separate list of actions proposed by students to resolve community conflicts—community gardens, a town watch, homeless shelters, a bookmobile, a shopping cooperative, a daycare center, more business, less traffic, a park, a clean-up day, a party, a porch sale. What is a good or peaceful community like? What is missing in a community full of conflict? What would my community be like if nothing was wrong? What can we do to make our community better?

**2.** Do an example poem on the board and have the class create the poem with your help in guiding questions and answers. Have a scribe write the composition neatly on the board as it evolves. In the list poem choose one of the ways to a better community. Embellish and aggrandize the ideas almost to excess. Try to maintain a realistic plan, but let the poem reflect the beauty and peace that it will offer to counter the conflict. Make sure the poem mentions the problem it is trying to fix, but let the solution predominate.

**3.** Have each student choose one community problem and describe the ways in which he or she will improve the community. The title can be selected after the poem is written, or students can use the theme as the title as a way of keeping themselves on track. Have students write these in paragraph form first, then rewrite for clarity later.

*What I Can Do to Make My Community Better*

The way I could help is by making gardens.
Painting murals on the garden walls. Plant seeds
so they can grow. Buy things for it, like soil, seeds,
watering cans, tools for the soil. The way I feel
about my community is sad because it is dirty, but
I'm going to help out. But after I'm finished I'm
going to be happy because it's clean. And that's
the way it is going to be. And that's the way I'm
going to help my community.

—Ramon Berrios (Grade 4)

## TOGETHER POEMS

Grades: 1–6

The "together poem" is an address poem meant to incite action. It expresses a need for community action around an issue that the public knows is a problem.

We've got to write this poem as one.
Together we can make it sing like sun.
Together we can fill it with helium balloons
of knowledge and language, rhyme and tone
and it can lift us off this page. Alone,
these words would turn us to dust and bone.
Let's write one together with our mouths
and our minds open just like this.
Let's make it tight as a fist, so good
we'll want to triple-write into flight
and out of sight. I say we've got to
triple-write into flight and out of sight.

—Aaren Yeatts Perry

By repeating a dynamic call to action such as "We've got to . . .," "Let's . . .," or "Together we can . . .," at the beginning of each line, the poet can create electricity between the class members and make them feel that they are already one body in agreement about a solution to a problem.

Have each student write a together poem calling for group action on the subject of his choice. From consuming a gallon of ice cream to building a literacy center to ending world hunger, the poem will detail in insightful lines the steps the group will take together.

## FURIOUS POEMS

Grades: 1–6

Together poems are related to a type of poem of address that McKim and Steinbergh call "fury poems." An example of a fury poem, says *Beyond Words*, "is 'The Fury of the Overshoes,' by Anne Sexton in which she addresses the child within her who struggled with the putting on and taking off of shoes. . . . Often children are encouraged to write poems on traditionally 'beautiful' subjects (e.g., flowers, friendships, etc.) whereas fury poems confer a structure which allows anger and conflict."[3] The ability to write about one's personal frustrations, if only in journal entries, hones a student's ability to articulate and distinguish between his own problems and the problems of the world.

**1.** Do a prewriting exercise in which you and the students make a list of things that make them "furious"—little things, big things, personal, social. McKim suggests writing a group poem called "The Fury of

______________," addressing one of these bothersome things. These poems can delve deeply into the subject, or they can be as short as the fury haiku.

*My Sister Haiku*

My sister screams loud.
She sounds like an elephant.
She is a fat rock.

—Nicole Caraballo (Grade 4)

**2.** Now make individual writing assignments of the same poem. Students can choose the thing that makes them the most furious. To minimize the likelihood of humor being misinterpreted as slander, encourage the selection of a thing rather than a person—the fury of a barking dog, homework, a dripping faucet, a runny egg, a cow lick, buttoning clothes, cleaning clothes, and so on. As with the other resolution-oriented exercises, request that the writers add to their ranting of dislike a line or two about their plan for fixing the problem, an "if-I-could-I-would . . ." or "one-day-I'm-going-to . . ."

## DREAM A WORLD POEMS

Grades: 4–6

Preactivity Class Reading: "I Have a Dream" speech by Dr. Martin Luther King, Jr.[4]

One well-known insight poem is the "dream poem" that Martin Luther King made into a speech. Kreidler suggests listening to King's "I Have A Dream" speech. It is also available on video.

After you have discussed it in the classroom, assign the class to write their own dream poem, but about a specific problem that they feel strongly about. Do one on the board in which you ask them to help you envision a drug-free neighborhood, or a crime-free city, or a universal health care system available to all! Explore what these would look like, who would be affected, what it would allow people to do, how it would be accomplished that could involve everyone.

A similar poem can be written by doing a prewriting exercise that involves daydreaming about one's future. This poem is listed in the Social Studies chapter under "Professions Personas."

*"Our hope is that one day all will be well; the illusion is that all is well today."*—Voltaire

## FIGHT POEMS

Grades: 4–6

This is a simple writing exercise that can be built upon, draft by draft. The intention here is for students to write down their understanding of the fight victim's pain. As a writing exercise this will build descriptive power. As a personal exercise it will contribute empathetic response and a social awareness that can help prevent fights. Before conducting this exercise, carefully consider the possibility that some of your students may have experienced physical pain or abuse.

**1.** Describe a professional wrestling match, a well-known boxing match, a martial arts demonstration the class may have seen, or even a dog fight. Discuss the critical difference between sports and uncontrolled violence against people. Make a clear distinction between the reasons that animals and people fight. How were the two fighters acting when they first approached each other? What did they say/do, if anything? How long did they posture before any punches were thrown or action taken? What did they look like when fighting? How did they move? Compared to what? Was anyone injured? How were they damaged? Did you see any weapons used? It is important to state clearly how the fight ended.

**2.** In the sample group poem on the board, describe a fight between two people using similes and metaphors: "Like two snakes/they hovered in tight circles/the tongues of their eyes/slithered through tight slits/tasting fear around each other./One pushed one/quicker than a cobra bite/rolling the victim in the dust/like a breaded chicken leg/about to be fried." If a mixed metaphor like that emerges, ask the writer about it and suggest possible edits after the first draft is complete. Try to describe the pain the victim experiences: ". . . cuts and bruises felt like fangs in meat. You could hear the venom bubbling."

**3.** Now have students write a description of a fight they have witnessed in which two people had a violent physical exchange.

**4.** Have students rewrite this interaction replacing the loser's name or character pronoun with *I*. Now the poet himself has fought, whether by choice or because he was attacked. Pass no judgment on either person or on the act of fighting. Simply describe the fight itself. Encourage the students to use as many of the descriptive tools they have acquired as possible in writing about these fights.

**5.** Make sure that the poet describes, at least as an ending, the physiological experience of the victim's pain.

## ABOVE IT ALL

Grades: 1–6

**1.** Dialogue with the class about tempers, emotions, and how easy it is for fights to break out in certain situations. Ask them to help you list some of things that can be done to keep a fight from happening. How do they feel when they have controlled a situation, when they can keep someone from getting hurt?

**2.** Now list some incidents that have caused trouble in your life or that almost caused a fight. Instead of fighting when these things were done to you, what did you do? How did you successfully defuse the anger? What are the five best ways to stop fights from happening? When you have compiled a list of responses and interventions, assign the poem.

**3.** Have students recount the same stories in writing. They can boast and brag and become as heroic as they want about not having to fight because they are "above fighting"—beyond violence, bigger than punching, stronger than threats, greater than guns. How many phrases can you and your class come up with that can give students a handle on violence?

*Violence*

I wish the whole world can stop all the violence,
So sit back in your seat and just keep quiet.
We are here to tell you what's going on,
and a brother's not promised to live his life long.
So let's take the time and combine
for us to live our lives for a long, long time.
When I was walking home last night,
I saw this couple about to fight.
So I stepped in and said, "That isn't right."
And I was proud of myself
because I broke up the fight.

—Jerjuan Mitchel (Grade 3)

## CHILL OUT POEMS

Grades: 3–6

Have two students who were in a conflict "chill out" (calm down) together in a separate room or in the corner or hall. Have them quietly discuss the incident and identify where things went wrong. Assign them the task of negotiating and agreeing on at least one, if not two or three, ways in which they could have resolved the conflict peacefully, without fighting.

To facilitate this, you may want to have a Chill Sheet with questions on one side and blank lines on the other ready at all times. You can give students a copy of this Chill Sheet when they are discussing the issues. It might be a question or two like the following:

We are in Time Out because we ______________________________

______________________________________________

This began when? ______________________________

______________________________________________

The real problem hiding here was ______________________________

______________________________________________

By doing that we were really trying to show ______________________

______________________________________________

How could you have done it differently? ______________________

______________________________________________

Who was hurt? ______________________________

______________________________________________

How much time did you waste? ______________________________

______________________________________________

What was gained? ______________________________

______________________________________________

What could you have done instead that you would have been more proud of? ______________________________

______________________________________________

Here is our no-trouble version of how we will do things differently:

______________________________________________

______________________________________________

If you have a mixed class or a high–low class, you may have developed a mentor or leadership program in which you can ask the older or more mature student to be the third-party mediator. Whether this is possible will depend on the behavioral norm in your class, but it can't hurt to try it a few times. I have seen it work in a situation where a same-age but more articulate student was able to help two who were more confused.

Make sure students understand the meaning of all the words used in your Chill Sheet by presenting it to the class in a discussion of discipline. Have them submit their ideas to you in writing on the form. Then have them take the finished form and rewrite it as a "Trouble Train" or "We're Above Violence" poem describing how they would nonviolently (without fighting) resolve the incident.

**1.** Another good writing challenge is to have students write the same in the present tense, as if it is happening now. Have them use the present progressive (*-ing*) form as much as possible to ensure that they are present with the story they're telling.

**2.** A third approach is a citation poem in which the psychology of the "bad guy" is turned on its head. A group poem is written about the two who acted wrongly (late and not paying attention), naming their mistakes without their help or participation. The group poem is not vengeful but uses the culprits as an example in a more creative way. The culprits pay more attention to this as they are barred from participation and made to watch. Be careful not to present this as either a reward or an attack, but as a warning for bad behavior. "Ms. Butterfield's class of well-behaved poets cites the misfits for . . ."

**3.** Finally, a hall spy poem can be used as an assignment for the student who is sent out into the hallway as a disciplinary measure. Certain schools do not allow this, but I have taught in many that do. One homeroom teacher sent a boy into the hallway during my workshop. I told him that his punishment did not excuse him from writing poetry and asked him to take a note pad and pencil and write a hall spy poem, observing and recording, with his mouth closed, all sounds heard in the hall. The resulting poem appears in the Human Values chapter.

## CONFLICT PHOTOGRAPH POEMS

Grades 3–6

Cross-curricula: Social Studies, Art

Preactivity Class Reading: "Death of the Ball Turret Gunner" by Randall Jarrell[5]

Pictures of conflict in newspapers or magazines are great tools for discussion. They are also an excellent component of any media literacy study. Cops, riot police, two neighbors yelling, two wrecked cars, a labor union marching, a woman with her head in her hands—these can be very evocative images to write about.

**1.** It doesn't take long to collect a stack of conflict photographs. Cut out enough for each student to have one. Make sure that the news story is still attached, but folded and paper-clipped out of sight, unless the caption beneath the photograph is descriptive enough.

**2.** Start by showing one picture to the class. Discuss the photographer's job. As an observer, this person has the important job of entering a conflict yet distancing himself from the conflict in order to document it, whereas a peacemaker, mediator, or negotiator has to step into the conflict in order to help create the solution. People in both professions have to be well informed about the conflict before entering it so that they don't jump to conclusions.

**3.** To that end, ask the students to help you list anything a student would need to know in order to solve a conflict. This is what William Kreidler calls a conflict Analysis Checklist.[6] It should include things like, "Who's involved? What did they do? How did they do it? What does A want? What does B want? What type of conflict is it? What are the needs of the parties?" Depending on your class, the list can be much more inclusive and descriptive of the conflict: Was this a conflict in which someone needed help a long time before this incident happened? Was the problem one that erupted just before the picture was taken? Was it an accident? If so, who or what caused it, and how could you have helped? If you were there, how would you have kept the peace, kept things from turning violent, or kept the conflict from happening?

**4.** Once you have the list of questions on the board for the students to reference, try a creative writing version of Kreidler's "Eyewitnesses" exercise. Here he suggests that you call students forward with their photographs and "interview" them with a microphone. Ask them to tell "our TV audience" what was happening in this picture.

**5.** Now ask students to write "If Only I Was There or If Only I Had Known, I Could Have . . ." poems (see Community Conflict Poems in this chapter) in which they tell the story of the incident in their photograph and explain how they could have helped keep violence from happening.

"I Witness" poems, also inspired by photographs, can be good practice for point of view, character, and voice of authority. Have students begin the poem with the words "I was there" or "I saw it with my own eyes" or "I saw the whole thing" or "And to Think That It Happened on My Street" or "From where I was standing I could see everything."

Rather than just rewriting the news story, have them transform it into a poem using the tools of description and authenticity: precise details, all of the senses, sequences of events, suspense, idiomatic expressions, fury, instruction, wonderment and speculation, postulation and wishes about what could have happened "if."

Another version of this same exercise can be attempted by having the students write a news story or poems of authority about a photograph before reading the caption. Then exchange the photographs and write an informed news story/poems as with the previous exercise. This is a good way to explore the issues of stereotyping and jumping to conclusions on the basis of what a situation looks like. You might even try mixing in with the "conflict" photos some that appear to be about conflict but are not.

## HISTORICAL CONFLICTS

Grades: 5–6

Cross-curricula: Social Studies

Preactivity Class Reading: "The Ballad of Birmingham" by Dudley Randall,[7] or "The Ballad of the Landlord" by Langston Hughes[8]

If one of your fifth or sixth graders is having trouble getting involved in a social studies assignment about a historical period, try assigning this project. During a unit on slavery, the "discovery" of the Americas, the Civil War, the Plains Indians, ancient Egypt, the battle of Hastings, or some other topic, you may want to try a poetry-writing version of another of William Kreidler's conflict resolution study ideas. He suggests having "each group research daily life in that period and report on the conflicts that young people faced and how they might have resolved them."[9] He makes the point that biographies of famous people often explain a lot about how individuals in our time can overcome or resolve conflicts.

Thus, the ballad. After students understand the conflicts that children of that era had to confront, have them create characters in their own image as if they were children in another era who had overcome a conflict. Did the child save everyone from a problem? Create and then solve his own problem? Fix a bad situation leaving almost all the parties happy but leaving some tragedy behind? What type of violence, if any, was perpetrated in this situation, and how was it disarmed?

The poem can be a ballad that makes the student out to be the hero who solved the problem. The A-B A-B A-A-B-A form of the ballad, as in those listed here, is easy to handle. The poem can be read or performed (memorized) for a class project. Have the writers consult the ballads listed here and others to expose them to the form.

> *"You say I contradict myself. Very well, I contradict myself. I am vast. I contain multitudes."*—Walt Whitman

## QUICK QUESTIONS POEMS

Grades: 2–5

Have students write down something that scares them or confuses them. They can take this opportunity to ask a question about a study area or a social or personal issue.

**1.** While they are thinking, write the questions and senses words from the Self-Questioning Guide Sheet (*who, what, where, when, why, how*).

**2.** Use one of the students' conundrums as an example, and write a line on the board for each question about it.

**3.** Have each student write a line for each interrogative expressing awe or amazement, or musing and wondering about the topic. Sometimes the questions reveal that they know a lot about something but are still afraid or confused by it or have new questions.

**4.** To expand on this in the rewrite, ask if they can add a line of description to each question. The brevity of the lines and the repetition of the questions alone can make this writing poetic.

*What Is a Friend?*

Is it a person who stands by you all the time?
Or talks behind your back?
Is it a person to whom you can take your problems?
Or is it a person to whom you take your problems
and they tell everyone?
Is it a person who likes you cause you buy them things?
Or is it a person who will like you for you?
What is a friend. . . .

—Lori Johnson (Grade 4)

*Tapestry*

What is life? Is it just an event
before death or is it a question
to be answered in the afterlife?
When you draw your last breath—
is it death or is it the continuation
of the tapestry of your life?
If you pull a string,
will it not unravel—
will that once beautiful woven picture
become a pile of colored yarn?

—Zubayda Muhammed (Grade 4)

## WHAT TO DO POEMS

Grades: 1–6

Children love solving problems and showing adults and each other that they know how to handle conflict. Another model for writing about problems as part of a process for dealing with them is to say in the poem what one should do in an emergency. This can be a boasting, confident poem declaring a student's preparedness for life. They can write it in the past tense if they have had some experiences in which they solved problems. If a student can articulate a strategy for resolving a problem before it happens, it's more likely that he or she will execute that strategy.

**1.** Even if they don't know the answers, it is helpful to prewrite some anything-goes questions. Have the writers help you create a list of possible troubles that could happen on their way home, at home, at school, and so forth.

**2.** For each item, have them give you a stanza of "The Things I Can Do When There's Trouble." Try the first few on the board before making the assignment. In this case, erase your ideas when you're done so that when the students are writing, they will use their imaginations.

**3.** Now have students select a specific number of the dangers listed on the board and write their own creative solutions.

Another approach to child safety is to write a group poem about when a child should (and should not) call 911, the emergency police and fire number. With grades 1 and 2, try writing a rhyming group poem. Students can dictate lines about when to use the emergency number, and the group can repeat a chorus about safety or trouble. As with all the early grades, make the poem short enough that when you read it back, the class can say it along with you.

A lament can help people who have no other recourse but to read a poem that makes them feel accompanied and understood in a time of helplessness. A good example is Randall Jarrell's war poetry. There is also W. B. Yeats's "The Lamentation of the Old Pensioner," a short poem about growing old that uses the usual "Ah" and "Oh" language of the lament.

This student produced a good list of questions but never got to the rewriting stage for the answers:

*What Can I Do?*

What can I do when I'm in trouble?
What can I do when I see double
What can I do when I'm stuck to glue?
What can I do when someone panics?

What can I do when someone runs away?
What can I do when I forget to remind people?
What can I do when I never see you?

—Christopher Smith (Grade 4)

## FORGIVE ME POEMS

Grades: 3–6

Preactivity Class Reading: William Carlos Williams's "This Is Just to Say"[10]

Many teachers and teaching poets use William Carlos Williams's humorous poem "This Is Just to Say" as a model. The irony in the poem is that he is apologizing for eating his host's plums, but he isn't really sorry. More, he goes on to expound on the excellence of their taste. Ultimately, the poem is an admission not of guilt but of pleasure.

**1.** In discussing this poem, also notice the line breaks. Do they help or hinder the poem? Where else might they be? As with any other poem that you might study, you can type the poem out in paragraph text and ask students to put the line breaks where they think they would work best. Then read the author's version and discuss what the author's intentions must have been. Was it a verbal emphasis for sound effects, for the visual effect on the page, giving inflection to certain words and thoughts?

**2.** In writing their own poems, students can explore the feeling of being sorry about doing something . . . but not really that sorry. Have them list things for which they have apologized but are not really sorry about and would do again.

**3.** Ask students to create unlikely scenarios in which they have taken, eaten, or in some manner used up something owned by another without asking, but enjoyed it so much that they simply leave a note, beginning with "This is just to say . . . ," which apologizes (without much remorse) and tells the person how much they enjoyed their things.

Try to get them to describe the senses inspired by the object, the feelings of unexpected pleasure they had, and some sense of sympathy for the person who will miss the objects.

*Sorry I Ate*

Sorry I ate your
Ice cream and messed
Up your kitchen. It

Was so good to eat
And I got a little too
Carried away. So I ate it
All up. I'm sorry I ate
Your icecream all
Up.

—**Orlando Poke (Grade 4)**

## SO MUCH DEPENDS ON POEMS

Grades: 3–6

In dealing with good interpersonal communication as a strength that can help avoid conflict, try having young writers do an exercise that uses the classic Williams's poem "The Red Wheelbarrow"[11] as a model.

**1.** Once the students have read the poem aloud and discussed it, have them give you a list for the chalkboard of things people "depend" on every-day.

**2.** Now have them focus the list on interpersonal qualities such as emotions and communication skills. When you have a sizable vocabulary from which to choose, have each student pick one quality about which to write a poem.

**3.** Challenge students to make their poem compare the quality they choose to something materially important in just a few lines. You may choose to do the same exercise with the vocabulary from any study area.

*Nelsonic*

So much depends upon markers and crayons.
Use them for projects, units, underlining.
In class, in other classes, other schools,
everywhere. Markers, crayons are everywhere.

—**Nelson Gonzalez (Grade 4)**

*The Black Anger*

So much depends on anger.
It is like a black hole sucking you in.
It feels weird.
The only thing I see is black.
Black everywhere and you can
lose your friend that way.

—**Rosemary Abreu (Grade 5)**

## PEACE CHEER

Grades: 2–5

**1.** Have a discussion about the types of weapons and violence the students in your class have witnessed in their neighborhoods and communities.

**2.** Do a re-visioning exercise in which you discuss what they would like to do about violence. Try to come up with at least five forms of violence or causes of it that they would like to change, ways they would like things to be, consequences for engaging in violence.

**3.** After you note these on the board and there is a sense of conviction in the classroom, ask for some jumprope rhymes, cheers, or chants. Write a few of these on the board. These are also used for selecting who is "it" in a game. "Easy meany miney mo/I know something you should know" or "Riddlee riddle ree/I see something you don't see and it looks like . . ." or "Easy meany macka racka whey 'n' rye 'n' dominacka. Icky chicken lollipoppin rum, pum, push!" or "Engine, engine, Number 9, chuggin down Chicago line. If you bring that gun/knife to school . . ."

**4.** When they are rewriting their familiar cheers and chants to reflect the school's safety rules and commonsense nonviolence, ask students to extend the chants to explain what people can do instead of fight, use weapons, or argue.

This is a poem of instruction, so it should be edited to include tight, sharp rhymes and punch lines that students can memorize.

One group of students working with a playwright in a violence-ridden neighborhood rewrote "Whisper Down the Lane" into a song called "Whisper Down the Gun," about the consequences of turning to violence. They took it to an after-school program and choreographed a dance to go with it.

## LAST WORD POEMS

Grades: 4–6

This is a self-confidence poem in which students can brag and vogue for a moment in spite of their problems. It is one of several verbal talisman or oral self-defense poems contained in this book. (The others are in the chapter on Human Values.) These playful "I'm O.K." chants will not stop a bullet or change the world, but they can help deter conflict by helping students keep their heads up and keep things in perspective. What secret power ending could be added to this poem that would help the author keep things in perspective?

*For Etheridge Knight*

My mom say I talk too much.
I don't get out and walk enough.
My dad say I sleep too much.
I dream of driving a jeep too much.
My brother say I sing too much.
I dream of getting a five-finger ring too much.

—Deonna Mears (Grade 5)

**1.** First have students write down their secret power. It can be a physical ability, great dreams, taste or appetite, vision, looks, tricks, knowledge of certain facts, even favorite objects that contain an unknown quality that is their secret power. Create enough examples so that each student can find one if they don't know their own yet. You may have already created such a list in the Human Values chapter.

**2.** Choose a student in the class who can be a model for this poem. Ask him to give you a list of the things that he is criticized for, that his family and friends complain about, even things that bug him about himself. Have him write his own secret power on the board as a last word: "But none of that can take away my . . ."

**3.** Ask the students to write their own self-defense poem that explains what people criticize them for. Give them some starter lines: "People might say I'm . . ." or "My friends all call me . . ." or "The world tries to get me down by saying that I'm . . ." Remind them that no matter what, they can have the last word. Suggest that the poets create an ending that declares one or two things that are great about them that cannot be changed or threatened or put down.

## NOTES

1. First published in "It's Never Too Late to Learn" by Dominique Roger, © UNESCO 1982, p. 1.
2. William Kreidler, *Creative Conflict Resolution* (Glenview, IL: Goodyear Books, 1984), p. 53.
3. E. McKim and J. Steinbergh, *Beyond Words: Writing Poetry with Children* (Greenharbor, MA: Wampeter Press, 1983), p. 92.
4. Martin Luther King, Jr., "I Have a Dream," in Kreidler, *Creative Conflict Resolution*, p. 80.
5. Randall Jarrell, "Death of the Ball Turret Gunner," in R. Ellmann and R. O'Clair, eds., *The Norton Anthology of Modern Poetry* (New York: W. W. Norton, 1973), p. 879.

6. Kreidler, *Creative Conflict Resolution*, p. 63.

7. Dudley Randall, "The Ballad of Birmingham" in J. Paul Hunter, ed., *The Norton Introduction to Poetry* (3rd ed.) (New York: W. W. Norton, 1986), p. 254.

8. Langston Hughes, "The Ballad of the Landlord," in Michael Spring, ed., *How We Live* (New York: Scholastic Magazines, 1977), p. 34.

9. Kreidler, *Creative Conflict Resolution*, p. 88.

10. William Carlos Williams, "This Is Just to Say," in J. Paul Hunter, ed., *The Norton Introduction to Poetry* (3rd ed.) (New York: W. W. Norton, 1986), p. 482.

11. William Carlos Williams, "The Red Wheelbarrow," in Richard Ellmann and Robert O'Clair, eds., *The Norton Anthology of Modern Poetry* (New York: W. W. Norton, 1973), p. 292.

# APPENDIX 1

# Glossary A: Tools to Do the Job

The following is an abbreviated list of definitions for poetry-writing techniques and elements of style.

**Alliteration:** The occurrence in a phrase or line of poetry of two or more words that begin with the same initial sound.

**Chant:** From the Latin word for "sing." In poetry, a short, simple melody in which a sequence of words or syllables is sung on the same note or at the same pitch. Also a rhythmic, monotonous call meant to evoke a celebrant emotional response in the range between speech and song.

**Comparison:** Stating or estimating similarities and differences by means, in poetry, of simile, metaphor, and other figurative language.

**Enjambment:** The continuation of one line or couplet of a poem to another.

**Figurative language:** Language that makes use of figures of speech; metaphorical, ornate language.

**Guide sheets:** Self-Questioning Guide Sheets and Poetry Critique Guide Sheets, two types of questionnaires for guiding discussion suggested in Chapter 2.

**Homonym:** Words that are spelled the same and sound the same but have different meanings.

**Homophone:** Words that sound the same but are spelled differently and have different meanings.

**Imagery:** Vivid descriptions using figures of speech to evoke mental images.

**Inner voice:** Speech heard internally but not spoken.

**Internal rhyme:** The rhyming of a word within a line of poetry with another word, either at the end of that line or somewhere in a subsequent line.

**Introspection:** Contemplative awareness of one's thoughts, feelings, and senses.

**Metaphor:** The transfer of identity from an object that a word usually describes to another object it describes only by comparison or analogy: "My head is a bass drum in a marching band today."

**Muse:** To contemplate deeply. Also, figuratively, a poet.

**Onomatopoeia:** A word that sounds like or imitates what it means: for example, *chomp, buzz.*

**Persona:** A character in a poem or play. The role one assumes or character one ascribes to oneself to portray one's intentions to others.

**Rhythm:** A metered or regulated flow of force such as syllables, consonants, breathing, or pauses.

**Scribe:** A person assigned to write down what is being said or to read it back, a poetry minute-taker.

**Simile:** A figure of speech in which two unlike things are compared or contrasted using the words *like* or *as*.

## APPENDIX 2

# Glossary B

The following is an abbreviated list of definitions for types of poetry, poetic forms, and idiom and genre names.

**Acrostic:** A poem in which certain letters, usually the first in each line, form a name, word, motto, phrase, or message when read in sequence.

**Address:** A poem that speaks directly to an object or person, as opposed to an anonymous audience or reader: "Ah, poetry, you synthesis of tears and laughter"; "Oh, heart, calm yourself."

**Approximation:** Poetry that mimics or resembles the style or technique of another poem.

**Ballad:** A narrative poem that is dramatic, romantic, or sentimental and consists of simple stanzas and a recurring chorus or refrain at the end of each stanza.

**Blues:** American jazz music evolved from African folk traditions, usually with a slow tempo and flattened thirds and sevenths, the lyrics of which appear in numerous permutations of quatrains, tercets, and parallels and deal directly or indirectly with pain.

**Chain:** In this book, a vocabulary-oriented poetry-writing exercise using the last letter of the first word as the first letter of the next word, and so on, with any poetic form.

**Cinquaine** *(SIN-kane)*: A five-line stanza, usually with a two-syllable title word, followed by a four-syllable line describing that word, followed by a six-syllable line containing action words, followed by an eight-syllable line of feeling or adjectives, followed by another two-syllable word for the title.

**Concrete:** Poetry formed to look like the subject matter, or a poem that can be spelled or phrased exactly the same way when written vertically and horizontally in a block.

**Couplet:** A unit of verse made up of two consecutive lines that rhyme or have a similar meter.

**Diamante:** A seven-line poem shaped like a diamond and structured as follows. The first line contains one word: a noun the opposite of the last word. The second line has two words: adjectives describing the first word. The third line has three *-ing* or *-ed* verbs about the subject in the first line. The fourth line has four words: nouns about the subject in the first and last lines. The fifth line has three *-ing* or *-ed* verbs about the subject in the last line. The sixth line contains two words: adjectives describing the subject in the last line. The seventh line contains a one-word subject: a noun opposite to the noun in the first line.

**Dream:** Poetry using imagery and story from dreams. Images or words from the subconscious that are used as metaphor or thematic content in a poem. A fantasy poem that is dreamlike.

**Epigram:** A short, witty, and surprising proverb, usually containing colloquial or idiomatic phrasing or metaphors.

**Epitaph:** A poetic memorial to one's life inscribed on a tombstone.

**Figure:** A poem written in the shape of an object.

**Found:** A poem created from found words or phrases that are either overheard and pieced together, physically cut out and assembled on the page, or by other methods combined intentionally to create a poem. (See Word Bag exercises.)

**Free verse:** In this case, a poem with no form restrictions.

**Fury:** Poems of fury "confer a structure which allows anger and conflict" (see the Human Values chapter).

**Group:** Group poems are compositions created by two or more people, either in alternating lines or, for example, in (alternating haiku and ageku) tankas as a team, a classroom, or a writing workshop.

**Haiku:** A nonrhyming poetic form of Japanese origin in which the first line contains five syllables, the second contains seven, and the third contains five. Usually relates an observation about nature or the passing of time, sometimes as a metaphor for other subject matter or content. The beginning of a tanka.

**Instruction:** A poem whose goal is to impart or profess knowledge in a literary voice of authority.

**Legend:** A popular story passed down via spoken word, usually about a famous folk hero.

**Limerick:** A rhyming and humorous poetic form in which five simple rules apply: It (1) is a story, (2) has a specific rhythmic meter or pattern (known as *anapestic*), (3) rhymes in an A-A-B-B-A pattern, (4) is funny, and (5) is (usually a mockery or satire) about a person with a made-up or real name. The last line should not only rhyme with the first but be a revealing and well-crafted punch line.

**List:** Poetry made of lists and given poetic life by unusual content or by oral presentation.

**Memory:** Poetry that uses memory as content, theme, or technique; as in dream poetry.

**Paean:** A joyful praise song.

**Parallel:** Poetry that repeats the same idea in different ways. A method of comparison indicating likeness or analogy.

**Proverb:** A short saying or colloguial expression that contains a profound truth, such as an adage or parable.

**Pyramid/volcano:** A figure poem in such a shape.

**Quatrain:** A stanza or poem of four lines.

**Renga:** A poetic form in which the tanka and haiku are used in repeating sequence in a longer poem.

**Senryu:** Another Japanese form of poetry in which the haiku loses its restriction of nature and seasons and can be about anything. Unless students craft the haiku assigned in this book to include elements of or reference to nature, they are technically senryu.

**Sestina:** A poem that uses the same six words repeatedly, each time in a different order, but always at the end of a line. The sequence is 123456, 615243, 364125, 532614, 451362, 246531. The last stanza has three lines, each of which have two end words: 2 and 5, 4 and 3, 6 and 1.

**Tanka:** A five-line poem comprised of a haiku (*hokku* or starting poem) plus two lines (*ageku* or ending lines) of seven syllables.

**Used to be/but now:** Form of figurative comparison poetry most notably developed by Kenneth Koch.

**Villanelle:** A form poem with nineteen lines consisting of five triple-line stanzas or *tercets* and a final quatrain of two rhymes, with the first and third lines of the first tercet repeating alternately as a refrain closing the succeeding stanzas and joined as the final couplet of the quatrain.

**Wish:** Poem based on various combinations of wishes.

# APPENDIX 3

## Chill Sheet from Chapter 9

We are in time out because we________________________________________________________________

_________________________________________________________________________________________________

This began when?____________________________________________________________________________

The *real* problem hiding here was____________________________________________________________

_________________________________________________________________________________________________

By doing that we were really trying to show_________________________________________________

_________________________________________________________________________________________________

How could you have done it differently?____________________________________________________

_________________________________________________________________________________________________

Who was hurt?________________________________________________________________________________

How much time did you waste?______________________________________________________________

_________________________________________________________________________________________________

What was gained?____________________________________________________________________________

_________________________________________________________________________________________________

What could you have done instead that you would have been more proud of?_________________________________________________________________________________________

_________________________________________________________________________________________________

Here is our no-trouble version of how we will do things differently: ______

______________________________________________

______________________________________________

______________________________________________

# APPENDIX 4

## Poetry Workshop Planning Checklist

Lesson name

Times per each phase of the writing exercise

Poetry tools used or introduced

Model poem

Visual/audio aids and supplies

Scribe

Student desk arrangement

Goals and objectives

Strategy notes

Questions

# APPENDIX 5

## Poetry Critique Guide Sheet

Any responses? Who can tell me what the poet means by . . . ?

How did that poem make you feel?

What do you think the poet who wrote that was feeling or thinking?

What was the feeling of that poem? Have you ever felt like that?

Opinions? Like or dislike? Understand? What about it?

Anything unusual about that poem? What did it mean?

Vocabulary? Content? Technique (tools)? Style (genre)?

What more would you like to know?

What made the poet write that?

Normal or irregular speech? Describe it. Characters?

Data about the authors or facts about the book.

Was that a head, heart, or belly poem?

# APPENDIX 6

## Self-Questioning Guide Sheet

What can I put in my poem?

Who, what, when, where, why, how?

Sight, sound, smell, feel, taste?

Are there things I would like to fix?

Line breaks, compound words, spelling?

Title, beginning, middle, end, name, date, room number?

Maybe I could add more . . .

Maybe I don't need that one word.

How does this look on the page?

How will this sound when I read it out loud?

Rhythm, movement, and emphases.

Loud? Quiet? Both?

What tools could I use to help me?

(These can be written in throughout the year.)

# Bibliography of Suggested Readings


Adoff, Arnold. *The Poetry of Black America: Anthology of the 20th Century*. New York: Harper & Row, 1973.

Adoff, Arnold. *My Black Me: A Beginning Book of Black Poetry*. New York: E. P. Dutton, 1974.

Interpretations of the Black American experience are presented in an anthology of 50 poems written by 25 poets.

Adoff, Arnold. *I Am the Running Girl*. Illustrated by Ronald Himler. New York: Harper & Row, 1979.

The excitement and thrill of running are portrayed in this series of poems.

Adoff, Arnold. *All the Colors of the Race*. Illustrated by John Steptoe. New York: Lothrop, Lee & Shepard, 1982.

Poems expressing ethnic diversity with compassionate illustrations.

Ammah, Charles. *Ga Homowo*. Accra, Ghana: Advance Publishing Company, 1968.

Arbuthnot, May Hill, and Shelton L. Root, Jr. *Time for Poetry*. Illustrated by Arthur Paul. 3rd ed. Glenview, IL: Scott Foresman, 1968.

A practical handbook to help children understand and appreciate poetry.

Banfield, Beryle. *Africa in the Curriculum*. New York: Edward W. Blyden Press, 1968.

Bohannon, Paul. *Africa and Africans*. Garden City, NY: Doubleday, 1948.

Brooks, Gwendolyn. *Bronzeville Boys and Girls*. Illustrated by Ronni Solbert. New York: Harper & Row, 1956.

A collection of emotionally filled verses that depicts the inner feelings of children who live in an urban setting.

Carruth, Hayden, ed. *The Voice That Is Great within Us: American Poetry of the Twentieth Century*. New York: Bantam Books, 1970.

Davidson, Basil. *The African Genius*. Boston: Little, Brown, 1969.

De Paola, Tomie. *Book of Poems*. Illustrated by Tomie De Paola. New York: G. P. Putnam & Sons, 1988.

An illustrated anthology of poetry from the classic work of Lewis Carroll to the contemporary poetry of Nikki Giovanni and Eve Merriam. Detail and wit are woven throughout the accompanying illustrations. A wonderful first for the beginning poetry reader.

*CHECK This Out: Highlights of Model Library Programs*. Department of Education, Office of Educational Research and Improvement. Pamphlet for sale by the Superintendent of Documents, U.S. Government Printing Office. (The hardback copy published in 1987 by the Department of Education is available and includes more information and funding sources.)

Provides models for successful library programs with an emphasis on Poetry Concerts.

Deutsch, Babette. *Poetry Handbook*. Minerva Press, 1957.

Describes many forms for poems.

Fage, J. D. *Atlas of African History*. New York: St. Martin's Press, 1958.

Fagg, William, and Margaret Plass. *African Sculpture*. New York: E. P. Dutton, 1964.

Gensler, Kinereth, and Nina Nyhart. *The Poetry Connection*. New York: Teachers and Writers, 1978.

This book offers many suggestions for poetry-writing sessions along with an excellent compilation of examples by adult poets and children.

Giovanni, Nikki. *Spin a Soft Black Song*. Illustrated by George Martins. New York: Sunburst, 1987.

Poignant, sensitive verses communicate the thoughts of Black children. Complimentary drawings convey the sensitivity of the text.

Gorer, Geoffrey. *Africa Dances*. New York: W. W. Norton, 1962.

Greenfield, Eloise. *Honey I Love and Other Love Poems*. Illustrated by Diane and Leo Dillon. New York: Crowell, 1972.

A collection of 16 short poems written with melodic rhythm about everyday childhood experiences. The expressive illustrations mirror the moving words.

Griaule, M. Marcel. *Folk Art of Black Africa*. New York: Tudor, 1950.

Hershkovitz, Melville. *The Human Factor in Changing Africa*. New York: Random House, 1958.

Hopkins, Lee Bennett. *On Our Way: Poems of Pride and Love*. New York: Knopf, 1974.

Seasoned Black poets coupled with the works of talented new poets offer a collection of 22 special poems on Black pride.

Hughes, Langston. *The First Book of Africa*. New York: Franklin Watts, 1965.

Hughes, Ted. *Poetry in the Making*. Boston: Faber and Faber, 1967.

A lively discussion of the process of writing poetry with several thematic areas described in depth.

Hunter, J. Paul, ed. *The Norton Introduction to Literature: Poetry*. New York: W. W. Norton, 1973.

Janheinz, Jahn. *Muntu, The New African Culture*. New York: Grove Press, 1961.

Koch, Kenneth. *Wishes, Lies, and Dreams: Teaching Children to Write Poetry.* New York: Chelsea House, 1970.

Koch documents his work as one of the first poets-in-the-schools. Using examples from children in the New York public schools, he lays out simple exercises for children.

Koch, Kenneth. *Rose, Where Did You Get That Red?* New York: Random House, 1973.

Koch suggests ways to use "great poems" as models for teaching poetry to children. Specific poems are included in the book.

Koch, Kenneth, and Stephen Judy, eds. *Scholastic American Literature Program,* Vols. 1–3. New York: Scholastic Book Services, 1977.

Kuskin, Karla. *Any Me I Want to Be.* New York: Harper & Row, 1972.

This appealing poetry's intent is to inspire the reader to become a creative writer. A mystical journey of discovery through 30 familiar creatures and things.

Larrick, Nancy, ed. *Somebody Turned a Tap On in These Kids.* Delacorte Press, 1971.

A collection of talks on teaching poetry to children.

Larrick, Nancy, ed. *Room for Me and a Mountain Lion.* New York: M. Evans, 1974.

Selected poems for children about places.

Larrick, Nancy, ed. *Crazy to Be Alive in Such a Strange World.* New York: M. Evans, 1977.

Selected poems for children about people.

Larrick, Nancy, ed. *Bring Me All of Your Dreams.* New York: M. Evans, 1980.

Selected poems for children about dreams.

Lewis, Claudia. *A Big Bite of the World.* Englewood Cliffs, NJ: Prentice-Hall, 1979.

Ideas for and examples of children's creative writing by age group. She discusses ways to integrate creative writing into the classroom curriculum. This is a lively and important work on writing with children by an experienced teacher and writer.

Lewis, Richard, ed. *Miracles.* New York: Simon and Schuster, 1966.

This is a moving collection of poems by English-speaking children around the world.

Livingston, Myra Cohn. *O Sliver of Liver: Together with Other Triolets, Cinquains, Haiku, Verses and a Dash of Poems.* New York: Macmillan, 1979.

An array of insightful poems on topics ranging from holidays to personal feelings reflecting the thoughts of youths.

Lopate, Philip. *Being with Children.* New York: Bantam Books, 1975.

A personal account of a poet's experience working in one urban school in the fields of poetry, theater, radio, and video. It describes some of the obstacles faced by visiting artists in schools, suggests writing ideas and ways to improve relationships between artist and teacher, and contains a very humorous chapter on trying to acquire grant money from large foundations.

Lopate, Philip, ed. *Journal of a Living Experiment.* New York: Teachers and Writers, Inc.

A collection of essays by poets and artists working in the schools through The Teachers and Writers Collaborative and the New York State Arts Council.

Lystad, Robert. *The African World*. New York: Frederick A. Praeger, 1965.

McKim, Elizabeth, and Judith Steinbergh, eds. *Beyond Words: Writing Poetry with Children*. Green Harbor, MA: Wampeter Press, 1973.

This is an excellent guide for parents and teachers.

Merriam, Alan. *A Prologue to the Study of African Arts*. Yellow Springs, OH: Antioch Press, 1962.

Nketia, H. J. Kwabena. *Music, Dance and Drama*. Legon, Ghana: University of Ghana, 1965.

Opoku, A. M. *African Dances: A Ghanaian Profile*. Legon, Ghana: University of Ghana, 1965.

Richardson, Elwyn. *In the Early World*. New York: Pantheon, 1964.

A moving and powerful statement of the potentials of teaching children through the arts. The examples of children's writing, art, and crafts are some of the finest ever published.

Roberts, John Storm. *Black Music of Two Worlds*. New York: Praeger, 1972.

Rothenberg, Jerome, ed. *Technicians of the Sacred*. New York: Anchor/Doubleday, 1968.

A range of poetries from Africa, America, Asia, and Oceana. This anthology of poetry and chant from tribal cultures around the world illuminates the oral tradition of poetry and reveals many techniques that modern-day poets have incorporated into their own writing.

Rothenberg, Jerome, ed. *Shaking the Pumpkin: Traditional Poetry of the Indian of North America*. New York: Doubleday, 1972.

Sandburg, Carl. *Rootabaga Stories (Poems for Children)*. New York: Harcourt, Brace Jovanovich, 1970.

Sandburg, Carl. *The Sandburg Treasury: Prose and Poetry for Young People*. Illustrated by Paul Bacon. New York: Harcourt Brace Jovanovich, 1970.

Stafford, William. *Writing the Australian Crawl*. Ann Arbor: University of Michigan Press, 1978.

A readable, illuminating, and inspiring collection of essays, interviews, and conversations by the well-known poet William Stafford, focusing on his process and philosophy of writing.

Summerfield, Geoffrey. *Voices*. Chicago: Rand McNally, 1969.

A wonderful anthology of poems and visual art in six paperback volumes. Selectively appropriate for grades K–12.

Sutherland, Efua. *Playtime in Africa*. New York: Atheneum, 1968.

Tufuo, J. W., and C. E. Donkor. *Ashantis of Ghana*. Accra: Anowuo Educational Publications, 1969.

Viorst, Judith. *If I Were in Charge of the World*. New York: Atheneum, 1981.

Poems for children and their parents.

Whitman, Ruth, and Harriet Feinberg, eds. *Poemmaking*. Massachusetts Council of Teachers of English, 1975.

A collection of essays by Massachusetts poets-in-the-schools.

Zavatsky, Bill, and Ron Padgett, eds. *The Whole Word Catalogues I and II*. New York: McGraw-Hill Paperbacks, in association with Teachers and Writers Collaborative, 1977.

An extensive and varied collection of ideas by teachers and writers for teaching writing to children.

Zweigler, Joy, ed. *Man, in the Poetic Mode*. Evanston, IL: McDougal, Littel, 1971.

# Index